Praise

'As someone who has stru‸
public speaking was always a major worry for me.
This book offers a fresh, practical approach that has
truly changed the way I think about speaking in
front of others.

'It focuses on simple, effective tips that help you
develop a clear message and structure, giving you a
solid path to follow. If you find yourself stuck getting
started or spend hours worrying about what to say,
this book provides a foolproof plan to organise your
thoughts and deliver them confidently. This shift in
focus has made presentations far more enjoyable and
much less stressful.

'Even in everyday conversations, I now use these
techniques to prioritise what's important, rather
than overwhelming my audience with too much
information.

'By practicing the strategies outlined, I've gone
from dreading public speaking to actually looking
forward to it. This is an excellent resource for anyone
looking to build real, lasting confidence.'
— **Nan Jones**, British Meat Processors
Association

'As a Chairman and CEO, with over forty-five years'
experience in the City and internationally, I've sat
through thousands of presentations at board and
professional level. If only more of the presenters had
followed Isobel's advice and guidance, everyone

would have benefitted, especially the presenters with more success. This book is a powerful summary of much of what she teaches – easy to read, easy to follow and full of tools and techniques that are proven and work.'

— **Stan Patey**, CEO, Termhouse
Corporate Finance

'Leading a business meant I had to speak publicly, which always felt like a hurdle despite my experience. Overthinking, talking faster than my thoughts and uncertainty were constant companions that truly took me out of my comfort zone. This book really flipped the script as it's packed with practical strategies that deliver instant results. It breaks down speaking into simple actions, so I can craft clear, impactful messages that actually land. Instead of dread, I now have a solid plan that brings confidence to every stage, from prepping to presenting.

'And it's not just for formal talks. These techniques have sharpened my everyday communication, making me more direct and effective. Implementing these methods has cut the stress and turned public speaking into something I genuinely anticipate. For any leader wanting to boost their communication and build real confidence, this book is a game-changer.'

— **Nils van der Zijl**, Vice President, Asset
Lifecycle

'A must for both seasoned presenters and those who are daunted by the thought of speaking in public.

'In this book Isobel brings together tools and techniques to not only structure your talk, but deliver it in a compelling, impactful way through real examples and stories. If you want to emotionally connect to your audience and compel them to take some sort of action or be captured by your presence, then this is the book for you.'
   — **Sharon Fennell**, Head of Talent and
      Leadership Development

'*Present With Presence* doesn't just teach you how to talk, it shows you why it matters. With warmth and wisdom, Isobel captures the fears and hopes of all of us who have to present.'
   — **Paul Russell**, Author, Design Thinker,
      Coach and Mentor

PRESENT
WITH
PRESENCE

Everything you need to plan,
prepare and deliver with
impact in any situation

ISOBEL RIMMER

R^ethink

First published in Great Britain in 2025
by Rethink Press (www.rethinkpress.com)

Front cover illustration and interior illustrations by Laura Féminier.

Contents

Foreword

As a politician, I'm all too aware of the impact my words (and actions!) have. When we look to influence policy, change people's views, inspire others to take up a cause, it's all through how we communicate, speak and present. In politics, communication is often under pressure – on the doorstep with voters and constituents, on TV and in radio interviews and, of course, when challenged by other members in the House of Commons. With limited time to prepare and generally 'on the hoof', I know how challenging it can be to speak and present well.

Through Masterclass Training, the company she founded thirty years ago, Isobel has worked with thousands of speakers from all walks of life – from graduates starting their careers to business leaders, politicians and CEOs around the world. She's coached people for TV, radio, conferences and boardroom pitches. Her bid presentation training has helped organisations win multi-million deals. I've seen her work first hand, and I know how she's helped so many people over the years.

She trains and coaches in how to present with impact, building people's confidence and enabling them to perform at their best, with presence and gravitas. Always with her clients' best interests at heart, she encourages them to go above and beyond, helping them look and sound brilliant. I've seen nervous presenters flourish and even the most experienced speakers step up to the next level.

I'm delighted that she's brought together her experience, knowledge and ideas in this easy-to-read and highly informative book. You'll have your own complete toolset, and she'll show you how to apply the techniques quickly and easily.

Everything she shares is about you and what you can do to become the best version of yourself. In her unique, authentic way, she will drive you hard, but it will always be worth it. She doesn't pull any punches, but as you'll find out, she wasn't a natural, confident speaker. She's been on the same journey and she knows what you might be going through.

Whether you are starting out as a speaker or already experienced, there's something for you in Isobel's book. Want to become a great storyteller? Handle nerves so that nobody knows you have them? Plan a powerful speech in less than ten minutes? You will learn all those things and much more.

If you want to have a powerful presence, be able to deliver with impact, whatever the situation, and light up a room – whether you're speaking in person or, as so many of us do today, online – you'll learn how, right here.

The Rt Hon Sir Ed Davey MP

Introduction

Everyone has to speak in public and present at some point in their lives. For the vast majority, the experience can be filled with fear and dread.

There's a word for it: glossophobia, a fear of public speaking.

It's estimated that over three-quarters of the population experience glossophobia,[1] sometimes fleetingly, but often as a full-blown panic attack. Indeed, more people fear speaking in public than they do flying, handling snakes or even death itself.

---

1 R Black, 'Glossophobia (fear of public speaking): Are you glossophobic?' Health Central (12 September 2019), www. healthcentral.com/condition/anxiety/glossophobia-fear-of-public-speaking, accessed 4 March 2025

Warren Buffett is often quoted on the importance of public speaking; that it is a skill needed for success – work on it and it's an asset that will last you fifty or sixty years, and if you don't, it will be a liability and you will always feel uncomfortable doing it.[2]

Whether you are starting out in your career and new to speaking at meetings, in presentations or pitches, at team briefings or project reviews, or whether you're established in a career in sales, consulting, politics, professional services or as a trainer and communicator where there is an expectation to be able to speak well and present with impact, this book is for you.

Public speaking is a broad topic – from talking to your colleagues at a team meeting to pitching to the board of a global organisation, to delivering the eulogy at a funeral or taking on responsibility for being best man or woman at a wedding, it comes in a wide variety of guises. My focus in this book is to help you develop in your professional career. I will show you how to plan and prepare so that you can deliver with impact and have a powerful presence – the magic that will make you stand out from the crowd.

I'll share tools, techniques and frameworks that will help you overcome your fears. Although I focus on business and professional work scenarios,

---

2   M Kulkarni, 'Warren Buffett explaining the importance of public speaking skills', YouTube (23 August 2012), www.youtube.com/watch?v=hHBRIzhbQ10, accessed 31 March 2025

everything I cover is relevant if you choose to move into politics, speak at a social event, produce videos as an influencer, attend a job interview, become a school governor or be active in your local church or community.

What can I bring you?

I've spent the last thirty years working as a trainer, speaker and business owner, and I have delivered thousands of training programmes, webinars and workshops. I've presented at numerous conferences and conventions, made multi-million-dollar pitches to boards and investors, and coached others to do so, too. I've trained politicians for TV and radio (including for the very first televised election debate in the UK), and on how to inspire their constituents on the campaign trail.

However, it wasn't always like that for me.

I remember as an undergraduate having my own terrifying experiences of public speaking. I watched as fellow students took to the stage with apparent ease and confidence, asking myself, 'How do they do that?' Putting myself forward at a recruitment panel, I forced myself to stand and present while my knees were knocking and my heart was pounding (surely someone must have heard...?), wanting to look confident, feeling anything but.

I was lucky. I learned how to present. I attended training courses. I read books. I watched others. I've been fortunate to learn from my colleagues, my trainers, other coaches, newsreaders, business leaders, politicians and many actors and voice specialists. I was filmed (and hated it) and learned from that. As a result, I realised that it's within everyone's grasp to be a compelling and engaging speaker – if you know what to do and are prepared to put in the practice.

Powerful Presence

Every day includes some form of presentation or speaking opportunity, often in person in workshops, in the boardroom, to large groups. For some, the opportunity is live on TV and national radio, in podcasts and virtually. We're all on TV now, navigating the trials and tribulations of Zoom, Teams, Google Meet, GoToWebinar and Webex.

The flagship programme of my business Masterclass Training, called 'Powerful Presence', was designed with my colleague, business expert and good friend Sharon Fennell. It evolved from a business need at a car rental company, where the MD was frustrated by how many ideas didn't make it to fruition. Not because they were bad ideas, far from it, but because the people with those ideas lacked the confidence and skill to present their full potential to the board. Our job was to create a programme that would give them the confidence and skill, along with the knowledge and, most importantly, the *presence* to pitch their idea and see it come to life.

More than just a presentation skills workshop, Powerful Presence brings together emotional intelligence (EQ) and how to hold the room – physically and virtually. It shows people the impact of kinaesthetic speaking (how we use space and connect with our audience in a physical sense), and how to rehearse and engage using stories and feelings. It covers what to do when you're faced with tricky questions or resistance from audiences, how to warm up your voice and manage nerves, how to dress to come across at your best and exercises for when you rehearse.

Powerful Presence has been described as life changing. It's not about us, the facilitators; the stars of Powerful Presence are the attendees. They're the ones brave enough not just to step, but to leap outside their comfort zone, trusting us to take them places they probably never thought they'd go. In so doing, they leave our workshop knowing exactly what they now need to do and with the confidence to make it happen.

What to expect from this book

This book brings together my coaching and training work in presentation and communication, and what it takes for me to be a speaker and professional presenter myself. It's based on my own experiences and the experiences of thousands of people, many of whom had the most severe strains of glossophobia. These are people who would have willingly had their fingernails pulled out rather than stand and present.

I promise you – if you follow the guidance in this book, if you put all that I share here into practice, if you summon up the discipline to do the things that I know work and take the time to rehearse and practise, not only will you learn to speak and present with impact, you'll find your own powerful presence too; your own magic that makes you the unique and special speaker you deserve to be.

Think of this as a recipe book you can dip into. Step by step, you'll become a confident and accomplished speaker, one with presence, while still being your authentic self. You will have to practise, of course, and I'll show you how. Just as it is when you create your own signature dish and favourite recipe, you'll find your unique style, your personality as a speaker, and become not just good, but great.

You'll learn how to handle nerves, look your best, and deal with tricky audience members. You'll thrive on challenging questions or resistance to your ideas. You'll become able to speak without notes. You'll cope when you don't know the answer to a question, and – trust me – you'll discover just how much fun it is when you overcome your fears.

Whether you're speaking in person or virtually, to small groups or large, I'm here for you. Let me take you on that journey. It may be a roller coaster – some bits a breeze, some more challenging – but I know that if I can do it, you can too.

As you go through the chapters, take time to reflect on the 'mindset, toolset, skillset' principles that I share at the end of each one. Practise the exercises and actions – it will be worth it, I promise you.

All that I have, I share with you. From my hands to yours.

Are you ready?

PART ONE
YOUR PERSONAL SATNAV

What is your goal when you are speaking in public? What does your audience want to hear? How do you want them to feel when they listen to you? Why are you speaking to them in the first place?

Without knowing exactly which direction you want to take your audience, how will you know if you've arrived? When you have a clear direction and are confident that the words you say will truly resonate with them, any nerves naturally start to disappear. No longer are you facing a pack of ravenous wolves, but a receptive, attentive and responsive group of people.

How do you prepare to deliver a presentation that your audience will remember and talk about? It's all here in Part One.

1
Where Do I Start?

Friday morning and my phone pings. The message reads, 'Hi, Izzy. Did you see *Question Time* on TV last night? We need to speak, urgently.'

I know what this is about. A politician or business leader, live on TV, didn't come across quite as well as they, or their party or organisation, hoped. It's my job to help and I love it. It's one of the things I'm lucky to do – helping people come across at their best when they speak in public.

It wasn't always like that for me. I remember how nervous I used to be when it was my turn to stand and speak or during those dreaded creeping death introductions round a roomful of strangers – do you go first and get it over with or wait and suffer in the build up? The sweaty palms, dry mouth, heart pounding. Yet others seemed so confident, no sign of nerves. Crikey – they even volunteered to speak!

This fear of public speaking – glossophobia – affects most people to a greater or lesser extent. Public speaking is incredibly stressful, and when you delve into our psychology as humans, it's no surprise. We're being stared at – go back thousands of years and that's a pack of wolves or another tribe ready to attack. Our brain is telling us to fight or flee. The adrenaline is pumping.

When I coach a speaker, the first question they ask is nearly always, 'How can I stop being nervous?' I promise them that we'll get to that.

My first question is different: 'How do you prepare?' This is typically what I get in response:

- 'I grab a few PowerPoint slides…'

- 'I put some notes together…'

- 'I write out what I want to say…'

'Yes, but how do you actually plan, prepare and structure what you want to say?' I ask.

Some reply, 'I tell the audience what I'm going to say. Then I tell them, and then I tell them what I've just said,' and look smug (or hopeful).

All very well, but *what* are you going to tell the audience? How do you know that's what they need to hear? Why are you presenting anyway? What's your goal, your outcome? What do you want your audience to go away thinking, doing, saying, knowing or, most importantly, *feeling* after you've spoken? How do you put your talk together and deliver it in the time you have? What do you do if the situation changes or things are running late? How do you know which slides you need? If indeed you need any.

That's when I get a blank look.

The journey ahead

If you don't know your destination, how will you know if you get there? If you don't know what your audience wants, how do you know what to say? Is it any surprise that you're nervous and tense when you don't know where you're going?

Try this. Imagine you're driving a beautiful car along an open road. It's a perfect day. There's no traffic, the sun is shining, you're on top of the world. Relax back in your seat, holding the steering wheel, and notice your position. Look where your hands are on the wheel. If you don't drive, imagine you're sitting in the passenger seat, cruising along, the soft top down.

Suddenly, you hit a wall of thick fog. You can't see more than a few feet in front of you. You brake hard. You lean forward. Look what happens to your hands on the wheel now. They're grasping it tightly. Your shoulders hunch up – you peer through the windscreen. You fumble for the fog lights. You may even turn down the radio or finish the hands-free call you were on. Your heart starts beating harder.

If you're the passenger, you'll tense up too. The conversation between you and the driver changes or stops altogether.

Then the fog lifts and you can see again. Clear, sunny, no traffic. You relax back, speed up and you're on your way.

Many speakers and presenters are in that fog. They don't know where they're going, so they're frightened of what might happen. They can't relax and enjoy the journey, and they have no way of navigating, no map, no satnav. They may rely on slides to guide them, and then those freeze and they're stuck, too.

This book will be your personal satnav. It'll show you how to plan, prepare and structure your message, and guide you in how to rehearse so that when you deliver your speech, your talk, your project update, your sales pitch, you'll know what to say and how to say it. You'll have a whole range of tools and techniques to deliver with impact, presence and confidence.

I'll share with you the secrets that give you charisma and gravitas so that you can hold the room, connect with your audience and be the speaker you perhaps dream of being today. Like many people I've trained and coached over the years, you might even begin to enjoy public speaking.

It starts here, with how you plan and prepare.

Start from the best position – believe in yourself

How do you feel about public speaking or presenting? Do you approach it believing in yourself? Do you feel you have the right to speak? Do you suffer from imposter syndrome, thinking that you have nothing significant to say?

Until you feel comfortable within yourself, you will struggle to win over any audience, whether you're facing an interview or promotion panel, briefing a team, sharing an idea with your boss or pitching for new work. This is not about being nervous. This is about how you feel about yourself.

There are three perspectives from which we can approach any communication, speech or talk. Ask yourself:

- Do I feel I bring value? Do I respect myself and the other person(s) equally?

- Do I believe in myself, but find myself frustrated or annoyed by the other(s)?

- Do I feel out of my depth – I don't really believe in myself, but the other(s) clearly know what they're doing?

You will likely have experienced all three.

This simple model puts you in control. It will help you be in the best position before you even start to plan or prepare your presentation. The perspective is your choice, and it *is* a choice, even though it may not feel that way. Stay with me on this.

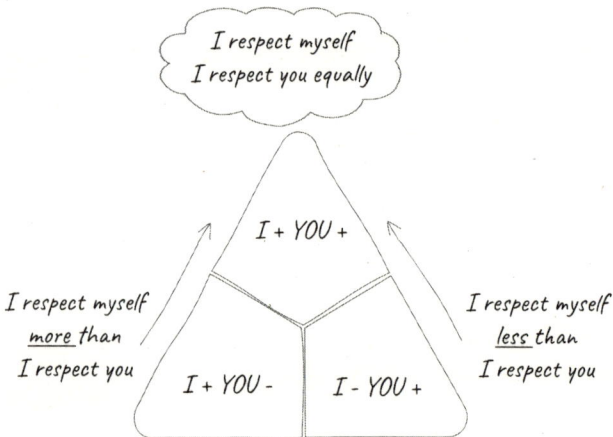

We can only legislate for ourselves. I can't control how you might feel about me, but I can choose how I enter our relationship and communicate and collaborate with you.

I+/You+

If I believe in myself, if I respect what I bring and I respect you equally, then I am at the top of the triangle.

This perspective is a position of mutual respect. I may be pitching to the board of a global organisation, but when I choose to connect from the I+/You+ perspective, what I have to say is of value to them. I may be nervous because it's a big deal, they're senior and experienced, and I know they will challenge me with tough questions, but I believe in my message, in what I bring, and I respect that they know what they're doing, too.

It may not be easy and I've got to get it right. I will if I respect myself and I respect them, too.

I+/You-

I believe in and respect myself, but I don't feel the same about you or the other person(s) I'm addressing.

When I find myself in this position – and remember, we choose our perspective, nobody makes us go there – it can be for various reasons. Perhaps I'm presenting to someone who has previously wasted my time, or I've gone to great lengths to prepare, invested hours only for them to cancel and say that it's not important anymore. Maybe I know more about the subject than they do – my technical knowledge is superior, but I'm going to have to explain, again, why we're doing things this way. Perhaps they don't respect my knowledge or experience. Maybe they won't listen anyway, so why bother?

I-/You+

I doubt myself, but I really respect and admire you or the other person(s) I'm addressing.

When I choose to enter the conversation or relationship from this perspective, I'm lacking self-belief. Do I have the right to be here? Can I speak up? The others know so much more than I do. In fact, why am I here at all? What do I bring?

What if the person I'm speaking to is very powerful and highly influential, and I'm going to be out of my depth? Maybe they put me down in the past or challenged me publicly, and everything in my bones is telling me to protect myself to avoid a repeat experience.

Almost certainly I'll over-prepare – and not use half of what I have. I respect myself less than I respect them.

The best, most effective speakers may have started from a position of I+/You- or I-/You+, but they've learned to move to I+/You+ so that when they deliver their message, they have the self-belief – not arrogance – and confidence that they bring something of value. Combine that with techniques to manage nerves and adrenaline, and breathe properly, and you'll be there, too.

How to do it

First, it's about awareness. Now that you know these three perspectives exist and I've given you language to describe them and a visual to picture them, it's your choice where you start from. You can make a conscious decision to be in I+/You+.

If you find yourself in I+/You-, where you respect yourself but not the other(s), here are a couple of things you can try:

Put yourself in the other person's/people's shoes. What challenges are they facing, what difficulties do they have? Create empathy, try to understand them. People say and do things for a reason, so be curious. Find out why. Don't just write them off.

Choose a different emotion. Our brains can't have two conflicting emotions at the same time. I can't dislike someone and like them.

I have worked with a man who is very demanding and always wants to know every detail. I would prefer he leave it to me and the team – we know what we're doing – and just back off, but he can't. He wants – no, he needs control.

Although it would be easy to default to I+/You-, I must not. I remind myself *why* he behaves this way. He's under pressure from his boss and he wants everything to be perfect so he looks good. He covers every detail, and some. He sets himself high standards and beats himself up when he doesn't meet them.

Outside of the work environment, he's a loving husband and a caring father. In fact, he's a very nice person and I now feel quite differently about him. I've moved from I+/You- to I+/You+.

What if you find yourself in I-/You+? Many speakers do, especially early in their careers when they feel less competent. They don't believe they have the right to speak. They tell themselves things like, 'I'm presenting to the CEO, what if I mess up? There's my career gone.'

To move from I-/You+ to I+/You+, here are a couple of techniques you can try:

- **Remind yourself why you are there**. It's because of the knowledge, expertise and skill you bring. If you're in an interview, tell yourself you *can* do the job – and now's the time to prove that.

- **Ignore your negative internal beliefs (NIBs)**. One of my trainers explains a lack of self-confidence through the lens of what he calls NIBs. I think of my NIBs as a parrot, sitting on my shoulder, squawking in my ear, saying that I don't deserve to be here, I'm not worthy, I don't know what I'm doing.

Nip your NIBs in the bud

My trainer gives his NIBs a name – Cedric. I call mine Polly. We tell them to get lost – I physically push Polly off my shoulder. I don't need her in my ear. I have the right to be here, I know what I'm talking about. Yes, I may be nervous, but I can alter that feeling, too. Reframe nervous energy as a feeling of excitement and the landscape changes. I'm here to speak, I'm excited and it's going to be great.

It takes time to shake off NIBs and my parrot does fly back, quite regularly. That surprises people. They assume that I'm always confident and in I+/You+, but even famous actors suffer from imposter syndrome. I remember doing an interview on national radio about greater representation of women at board level. I knew I would be up against a difficult opponent and Polly was loud in my ear as I entered the studio, but I sent her away and enjoyed the debate.

Recognise what this inner voice is – a NIB – and tell it to get lost – or go stronger with your language if that helps. Polly has been sent flying on many occasions with some ripe words ringing in her ears…

Reframing your mindset

Be aware that you can move rapidly between the three perspectives, so be ready to get back to I+/You+ when it happens.

I was organising a meeting with the CEO of a very large financial services organisation. I know him well, socially as well as professionally, and although he is a big and influential name in the market, I feel perfectly comfortable working with him. I am naturally in I+/You+.

However, as his PA and I struggled to find a mutually convenient date to meet (my diary being as tricky as his), she was getting frustrated. At one point, she sighed and said, 'He is very busy, you know, Isobel…'

In a matter of moments, I experienced two different emotions. Firstly, I went to I+/You-. I was thinking, 'He's busy? So am I!' Annoyance, frustration, don't speak to me like that.

In the next moment, I was at I-/You+. I know he's busy. He's the CEO of a massive organisation. He's a huge name; he knows much more than I do…

I had to reframe my mindset, get back to I+/You+, and fast. In my head, I considered the PA's position. It must be a nightmare, trying to organise his diary, no wonder she gets a bit fractious. I had to show empathy.

'I know, it must be very tricky managing all his commitments,' I said. 'You do a brilliant job. I'm sure we'll find a suitable slot.'

That's exactly what we did.

FROM MY HANDS TO YOURS

Mindset

- Make sure that you are consciously in I+/You+ as you prepare to present or speak.
- If you find yourself slipping towards I-/You+ or I+/You-, check yourself and consciously move back to I+/You+.

Toolset

- Think of your talk, presentation or speech as a journey. Just as you would plan a trip, check the map and make sure you have everything ready.
- Identify your NIBs and give them a name if that helps. Tell them to get lost or whatever phrase works for you.

Skillset

- Create opportunities to get into I+/You+, and not just when you're speaking. If you find yourself in I-/You+ or I+/You- in a meeting or when talking to someone, acknowledge that you're there. Give words to the feelings and emotions that you have. Park them and consciously move to I+/You+.
- You'll find that with regular practice, you will become very aware when you're *not* in I+/You+ and build strategies to use, in the moment, to get you back.

2
It's All About *Them*

This may sound unconventional, but let's get one thing straight: when you speak or present, it's not about you. It's about your audience. In fact, it always has been about them.

In this chapter, I want you to embrace a mindset that focuses on your audience's needs, desires and experiences. Picture this: instead of standing in the spotlight, you're stepping back and allowing that light to shine on them. They are the reason you're there.

When you shift your focus to them, you open a door to deeper connection. What challenges do *they* face? What questions do *they* have? What insights can you offer that will help *them*?

Keep this in mind. Think audience. After all, the true measure of a great speaker is in the connection you make.

It's not about you, it's about them.

Your audience

I use the word 'audience' in its widest sense. You might be speaking to one or two people on Zoom or Teams, presenting at a conference to several hundred people, on national radio or TV broadcasting to millions of listeners and viewers. Whatever the situation, remember, you're there to *help your audience*.

Reframe – it's not about you – it's about *them*:

- You might have to convince them of your skills at a job interview. They need to hire someone.

- You're there to pitch your products and services. They need to buy something from someone.

- You're updating your team on a project. They need to know.

- You're delivering the eulogy at a funeral. They're there to remember the life of someone you all cared about.

- You're making a speech at a wedding. They're there to celebrate a happy event.

Your audience wants you more than you may realise. Shift the spotlight from you and on to them.

When we choose to put our audience and their needs first, the dynamics change. What we say is for their benefit, not ours, and when we care about them and are clear on what they're going to gain from our presentation, we can let go of our fears.

Have your audience's best interests at heart

Charles H Green is the author of *The Trusted Advisor*,[3] *Trust-Based Selling*[4] and *The Trusted Advisor Fieldbook*[5] – all excellent and worth reading. He's also the brains and creator behind the brilliant Trust Equation. From my experience of coaching speakers, especially those at the higher end of the glossophobia spectrum, the Trust Equation is a great tool to overcome your fears and build trust and rapport with your audience.

There are four variables in the Trust Equation. On the top line – the numerators – you have credibility, reliability, intimacy, and in the denominator, self-orientation.

---

3   CH Green, DH Maister, R Galford, *The Trusted Advisor* (Simon & Schuster, 2002)

4   CH Green, *Trust-Based Selling: Using customer focus and collaboration to build long-term relationships* (McGraw Hill, 2005)

5   CH Green, AP Howe, *The Trusted Advisor Fieldbook: A comprehensive toolkit for leading with trust* (Wiley, 2011)

$$Trustworthiness = \frac{Credibility + Reliability + Intimacy}{Self\text{-}Orientation}$$

Credibility is about what we say, what we know, the words we use. People trust us because we 'know our stuff':

> 'I can trust Jan; he's an expert on sustainability and I've read many of his reports. They're first class.'

We will nearly always present because we are the expert or the right person to speak about a particular topic. If you're asked to speak on something you know little or nothing about, you might want to think again.

Reliability is aligned with actions – what we do. We build trust with our audience by being dependable, doing what we say we will do. That means turning up when asked to, fully prepared, and delivering our presentation or topic (not something else) within our allotted time.

Build a reputation of being the one who never runs over. Speakers who are reliable and fully prepared, who deliver what is asked of them, are an absolute pleasure, believe me.

'It's always a delight to have Saima speak
at our events. Not only does she know what
she's talking about (credibility), but she
keeps to the time, makes sure that her talk is
engaging and answers our questions in detail.
She checks with us before the talk to make
sure the technology works, and her slides are
beautifully presented, clear and engaging.'

Intimacy is to do with how safe others feel when they
interact with you. Are you prepared to show some vul-
nerability and emotional candour? Can you use emotion to convey how you feel? Is your self-awareness
strong and your empathy high?

'It was fascinating to hear Sanjay talk about
the challenges he faced when he first joined
the company. It must have been incredibly
tough for him, but listening to him talk about
his experiences and the way he shared how it
was has really helped me to see how we can
support new hires much better. I appreciate
him being so open and honest.'

Self-orientation, the denominator in the Trust
Equation, is all about whose best interests you have
at heart. If your self-orientation is perceived by your
audience as high, then it's all about you. When it's
perceived as low, you are seen to have *their* best interests at heart. Believe me, an audience knows whether
you do or you don't.

'What I really appreciated was the work Sharon put in before our conference. She took time to understand the challenges our delegates faced and checked to make sure that her examples and stories would work for their industries. Nothing was too much trouble, and she made sure everyone had a fantastic experience.'

You know the importance of being in I+/You+, and from now on, you can reframe how you feel about your audience. It's about them, not about you. Whenever you are asked to speak to an audience, remember you're there to help them.

Why are they here and what do they need to know?

Now we are thinking about our audience (and less fixated and focused on ourselves), we can see things more clearly from their perspective – what I call 'getting into their shoes'. Why are they here and what do they need to know?

Whenever I coach a presenter – whether it's a politician on the campaign trail, a CEO at a company town-hall event, a sales team pitching, someone presenting at a board meeting – I get them to think first about their audience. Who are they? What are they like? What do they worry about? What do they want to see? What do they need to know? The more you understand your audience and their world, the easier it is to connect, the greater the rapport, and the more effective your presentation will be.

Audiences are diverse – young, old; different life experiences, preferences, communication styles. Not only do you need to think audience, you need to flex and adapt to a range of different requirements. You may have to balance rich detail for some people with a summary for others – there will be audience members who want everything, others who just want the key facts. Some are impatient to get straight down to business, while their colleagues enjoy anecdotes and social chit chat. Humour may work, but not with all (my advice: only use it if you're naturally funny, and if in doubt, leave it out).

A good speaker, one who's worked to hone their skills, taken the time to refine their approach and acted on feedback, will know that to be a great speaker, they must flex and adapt to their audience. Ask yourself: 'Why are these people here? What do they need to know?' In later chapters, I'll show you how you ensure what you say gives different audience members what they need, but the first step is to see things from their perspective.

The power of the radar

I remember my father talking about when his brother Ian, a farmer, took his driving test. It was in a remote part of Scotland and Ian had to show the examiner he could do a right-hand turn safely. The examiner asked him to imagine traffic coming the other way and prepare to turn, but there was no traffic and Ian, being a practical type, simply couldn't imagine there being any. The odd tractor, maybe...

In other words, he was being asked to do something that he couldn't. Not everyone can imagine things.

I worked recently with a senior lawyer and that story came back to me. He is a subject matter expert in his legal field who was to pitch to the board of a major new client. I was there to make sure the pitch was a success and he won. It was a big opportunity and the pressure was on.

As we prepared, I asked him to get into the shoes of his audience and think about what worried them, their likes and dislikes. He stared at me blankly – he couldn't imagine. Just like Ian, he needed something more concrete.

Enter my radar.

Consider a radar at an airport and how planes come on to it, land, and then move off. Big bleeps, little bleeps. Like air traffic control, we too have radars: issues that are bleeping and constantly changing.

You might have a pressing matter you're dealing with right now – a big bleep. My colleague's house has flooded – she can't think of anything else. Alternatively, there may be something not yet on the radar, but it will be bleeping soon – Christmas is coming, tax returns are due, you must get the car insured.

When someone cancels a meeting, it's because something else is bleeping on their radar that right now is more important than the meeting. When my hairdresser cancelled my appointment (a disaster for me), it was because her daughter was admitted as an emergency to hospital. It was a big bleep on her radar at that moment. Nothing else mattered.

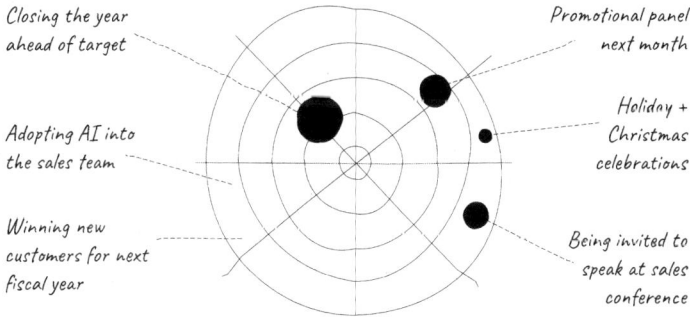

Closing the year ahead of target

Promotional panel next month

Adopting AI into the sales team

Holiday + Christmas celebrations

Winning new customers for next fiscal year

Being invited to speak at sales conference

What might be on my divisional manager's radar?

Using a radar is a powerful way to see things from your audience's perspective and understand their priorities, interests and concerns right now. You'll never know their needs exactly – things can and do change, but taking a few minutes to look at their radar will make a big difference as you prepare your presentation.

The starting point is to think about what *could* be bleeping on their radar and to look at it from two perspectives:

- Tangible, measurable things that you can probably talk about
- Intangible, harder to measure things that you probably can't or won't talk about

Tangible, measurable issues: AKA results

What are the priorities your audience is facing? What are the metrics, key performance indicators (KPIs) or objectives they must deliver against? How do they demonstrate success in their role? What are they measured on? How do they know if they're on track? How does their boss know? What are the big bleeps they must deal with right now?

In the diagram above, I've captured on the left-hand side results that might be on my boss's radar. In most business presentations, you can put a number against these results. It might be pressure to grow revenue (£$€), increase market share (%), reduce costs ($£€), deliver sales targets ($$$), manage cash flow (£$€), recruit teams (#), retain talent, deliver projects on time, come in under budget, win pitches, save lives. It might be all of those.

What gets measured gets done, so tangible things that your audience is measured on – the results – will bleep. If it's a high priority, a big bleep, it will be the focus of their attention right now. It doesn't matter whether you think it's a big bleep, it's what *they* think. If what you've got to talk about in your presentation can help deal with it, you'll be welcome.

I was running a training session for a multi-national leasing company. Just after lunch, there was a knock on the training room door and we were told that the company had gone into administration and everyone had to leave the building, immediately. As my team and I gathered our things, the employees filed out, some grabbing pot plants and computers on the way. At that moment, their radars had one big bleep: were they going to get paid?

It was the one thing bleeping on our radar, too.

Intangible, harder to measure: AKA personal wins

It's not just about tangible metrics and results. Other things bleep, too. Less tangible and more based on emotions, I call them personal 'wins'.

Your audience might be worried about how secure their job is, whether they have the influence they'd like with colleagues. They may be worried about the future. They may like to be right, seen as the go-to person. Can what you're going to talk about address their concerns?

Perhaps they worry that you're an expert, and they're not. Will they look foolish if they ask a question? Will colleagues think it's dumb and snigger? Are they just looking for an easy life, and coming to your presentation beats doing an afternoon's work? Are they a fudgel (a wonderful word for someone who pretends to work when they're not actually doing anything at all)?

Your audience may be concerned about an elderly parent who's moved into a care home or the messy divorce they're going through. They won't share their wins as openly as they might share their results, but they're as important – sometimes even more so – and you need to relate to them in your presentation in some small way, even though they may be left unspoken.

On my diagram, I've captured examples of personal wins on the right-hand side.

Create a radar for your audience

To help you prepare for any speech or presentation, draw a simple radar like the one in my diagram and plot the things that you *think* are bleeping for your audience. The bigger the bleep, the nearer to the middle of the radar, the higher the priority.

Start with the measurable results. I put them on the left-hand side of my radar. You'll never know everything about your audience's results, but you can probably identify at least three or four bleeps – priorities – based on what they're measured on and the challenges they face.

Now think about your audience from a more personal perspective, their wins. I capture these on the right-hand side. What's the political situation in their business? Are they looking to have greater influence in their organisation? Are they wanting a quiet life until they retire? Do status and reputation matter to them? If you know your audience well, you might add wins outside of work: caring for family members, an illness, moving house. Using a different colour for results and personal wins helps make your radar diagram clearer.

Now step back. What's emerging? How does what you will present on or speak about connect with their results and wins? Are you introducing something that isn't even yet a small bleep? If yes, why would they listen? What value would they see in what you say right now?

If you can't connect what you're going to talk about to something on their radar – preferably to something large, important and close to the centre – don't be surprised if they seem disinterested.

I was working with a senior partner in a consulting firm. I could see that his team would benefit from training in business development and spotting sales opportunities, but his head was elsewhere. He was concerned about his pipeline of current deals and how quickly he could close them. Revenue was the big bleep; training wasn't even close. In his mind, he didn't have time to put his people through a training course – they had to be out closing deals.

To get time in his diary to present my ideas, I had to connect on what mattered to him at that moment. I explained that I was aware that growing the pipeline and being able to move deals quickly through it was a high priority and that I could potentially help him. That got his attention. He wanted to know how. The next day, we were talking about the training programme. Now training was on his radar and mattered to him, and yes, he went ahead with it.

Spend a few minutes creating a radar and you will build greater awareness and empathy (remember the intimacy from the Trust Equation). You get an opening into your audience's world and, in so doing, shift your focus on to them.

It's said that you must walk a mile in someone's shoes to understand them. Harper Lee put it more beautifully in *To Kill a Mockingbird* as Atticus Finch talks to his daughter.[6]

---

6   H Lee, *To Kill a Mockingbird* (William Heinemann, 1960)

'If you can learn a simple trick, Scout, you'll get along a lot better with all kinds of folks. You never really understand a person until you consider things from his point of view... until you climb into his skin and walk around in it.'

What happened with the lawyer I mentioned earlier, the one who found it impossible to imagine? We drew up a radar and captured all the things that his prospect client (the board members of a large agricultural firm) would be measured on – results – and what they might be concerned about personally – their wins. With the radar to help him, the lawyer could get into their shoes (even though they were green and made out of rubber while his were polished black) and see things from their perspective.

Glossophobia doesn't automatically disappear when we reframe that we're there to help our audience, but this is a step along the way. In the chapters ahead, I'll share tools and techniques to help you manage nerves and boost your confidence to be able to deliver with presence, but start by taking the pressure off you. Remember, when you present something – anything – you're there for your audience's benefit. It's not about you – it's about them and what they will take away.

Putting yourself in your audience's shoes and thinking about what's going on in their world will help you to connect on the issues that matter to them. Make it a habit: spend a few minutes creating your radar, capturing the results and wins of your audience. Better to do that and build a picture than not have a clue. Even if you find it difficult to imagine – like Uncle Ian and my lawyer client – you can build a radar and step into your audience's world.

FROM MY HANDS TO YOURS

Mindset

- Recognise that when you are speaking – to any audience, large or small – you are there for them. Yes, you are the speaker, but it's not about you; it's about what they will take away from listening to you. Shine the spotlight on them and take the pressure off you.

Toolset

- The best speakers build rapport and a sense of trustworthiness with their audiences. Use the Trust Equation to ask yourself:
    - Credibility – will it be clear that I know what I'm talking about?
    - Reliability – can I consistently show that I do what I say I will do?
    - Intimacy – how can I make my audience feel safe with me? Am I prepared to show some vulnerability?
    - Self-orientation – do I come across as genuinely having my audience's best interests at heart (low self-orientation) or do I come across more interested in what matters to me?

- Draw up a radar for the person(s) you will be speaking to and spend time thinking about what's going on in their world. Consider what their priorities might be, their results, and capture them on your radar on the left-hand side. The bigger the bleep, the more important that result is for them right now. Then look at what matters personally, their wins, and capture those on the right-hand side. These will be less tangible, but they are critically important in understanding what really matters to the people you're speaking to.

Skillset

- Get into the habit of using the Trust Equation by observing how other people – colleagues, customers, suppliers – make you feel. When you experience rapport and trust, explore why and check against all four aspects of the Trust Equation. You will then see what works, and why.

- Create a radar for people you work with, and not just when you do a presentation or speech. Make it a habit so that it becomes something natural and authentic that you can do easily and quickly. When you use it with people you know well, you can check in to see how accurate you were. This will help you to become skilled and build your confidence.

3
Planning And Preparation – The Secret To Success

There's an old saying: 'We never find time to do things right; we always find time to do things twice.'

How often do we hear someone say, 'I don't have time to prepare...'? The truth is, though, that putting in the time to plan and structure your presentation pays off in ways you might not expect. It's not just about knowing what to say; it's about connecting with your audience, easing your nerves, reducing stress and coming across at your best. It is *the* secret to success.

Don't be fooled by those effortless speakers who appear to just wing it; those TED talks that feel like fireside conversations. They're often the result of years spent honing presentation skills, lecturing in universities, speaking at conferences, and rehearsing countless times. It's a similar story for comedians – the laughter and jokes may flow freely, but the hours of practice and rehearsal go unseen.

When the British comedian Sir Lenny Henry lived near Windsor, he'd rent a small theatre in the old fire station, offer cut-price tickets to local folk (it was brilliant, we'd go whenever we could) and rehearse his shows before going on tour. The polished performance we'd see months later was the result of hours spent perfecting timing, testing jokes and fine-tuning every detail.

The secret to a successful presentation? It's all in the planning and preparation. Yes, you need stories, perhaps some slides and, of course, engagement with your audience, but you must invest in preparation.

In this chapter, I'll share the first steps in my simple yet powerful method, a recipe you can follow. Stay with it and you'll find that you can create any presentation. As you get familiar with it, you'll put your own spin and personality on things and be able to do it easily in minutes – and I mean that. A client who could be doing three or four different presentations in a day, from national radio and TV broadcasts to after-dinner speeches, said to me when I showed him my method, 'Thank you, Izzy. If only I'd known this years ago, what a difference it would have made. Using this, I've got my weekends back!'

You can thank me later…

Know where you're going

As I walk you through my method, have a piece of paper and something to write with handy. An A4 sheet is ideal, or if you have a reMarkable or an iPad or sketch function on your computer, use that.

You can do this landscape or portrait (years of using a flip chart mean I tend to stick with portrait, but it doesn't matter). At the top of the page or sheet, write 'Audience'. At the bottom of the page, write 'Outcome', and in the middle put the title of the topic you're going to be speaking about and draw a circle around that.

From the previous chapter, you can use your radar and capture, under 'Audience', the results, wins and needs of the people you're going to be speaking to.

AUDIENCE:

TOPIC

OUTCOME:

Let's take an example and work through it together.

You are presenting a business plan with the aim of securing funds and resources from an organisation to run a critical project. Your audience is the senior board including the finance director. They are demanding people, quite impatient. They will want you to get to the point and what you're asking for to be realistic, accurate and considered. They'll want to know how much the project will cost, how long it will take and when they can get their money back. In fact, that's what nearly all boards want to know about any project.

They'll probably interrupt you with their questions (even if you ask them not to). They'll want to be sure your facts and figures are correct, and that you'll deliver on time and on budget. You must be concise, efficient and on top of your work.

Step 1

You've already got useful information from the work you did on your radar. Capture what you know about your audience at the top of your sheet.

This presentation isn't about you, it's about them. What's bleeping on the left-hand side of their radars? Delivering results? Revenue and growth? Keeping costs under control? Managing risk?

On the right-hand side, what's bleeping on their personal wins? Being in control and visibly competent? Recognised as experts in their field? Seen by colleagues and peers as knowledgeable and successful?

Capture everything that will help you understand your audience better and see things from their perspective.

Step 2

Now let's move to the topic. I'm going to give our presentation to these leaders the title of 'Project Resource'. Write your topic or presentation title in the middle of the page and draw a small circle around the words so that they stand out. Choose your topic title – briefing, sales pitch, project update – as appropriate.

The title might change. Perhaps you start with 'Team Briefing', but then as you build your presentation, you find 'New Way of Working' is more accurate. Edit as you go along.

Step 3

Move now to the word 'Outcome' at the bottom of your page. For the first few times you do this, write down these five words:

- Think
- Feel
- Say
- Do
- Know

Now ask yourself, 'What do I want **this** audience to go away *thinking, feeling, saying, doing* and *knowing* as a result of my topic?'

When you plan this way, answer each one of the five variations of this question. Doing this gives you greater clarity on what you must talk about and what you could talk about.

As you become familiar and confident with this approach, you may not need all five – you might only focus on three or four, but for now, work with all five. Here's my secret – always keep the 'feeling' one. What do you want your audience to *feel*? A famous quote, often attributed to the author Maya Angelou, says: 'I've learned that people will forget what you said, people will forget what you did, but people will never forget how you made them feel.'

As you capture what you want your audience to go away thinking, feeling, saying, doing and knowing, write it down as though you are speaking directly to them, using the word *you* not *them*. For example, I want you to:

- **Think** that this is a well-thought-through project plan

- **Feel** confident in me as the project lead

- **Say** that you will approve the budget and we can proceed

- (**Do**) Release the funds and sign off the budget request

- **Know** we are a strong project team and will deliver on time and on budget

AUDIENCE: <u>BOARD + CFO</u>
      Facts, Figures, Accurate Data,
      Efficient, Pragmatist, Risk,
      R.O.I, Payback Investment

> *Secure Project*
> *Resources*

OUTCOME: *Think*   *Well thought through*
      Feel   *Confident in you*
      Say   *Approve budget + proceed*
      Do   *Sign off*
      Know   *We will deliver on time + budget*

Focus on outcomes

This approach will help you focus on the *outcomes* you want from your presentations. Being clear on what it is you want your audience to think, feel, say, do and know and relating these to what is on their radar (results and wins) will guide what you say and ensure your presentation meets their needs.

Think of this as your presentation satnav system. You know where you're going (outcomes), you know those outcomes are important for your audience (results and wins) and you can see the road ahead. You may face challenges along the way, but you've got a plan to see you through, and not only do *you* know where you're going, *your audience* does, too.

The more you use this approach, the more quickly and easily you will build your outcomes. I've shared some examples below to help you. For each one, we're asking, 'What do you want *your* audience to go away thinking, feeling, saying, doing and knowing as a result of what you're going to talk about?' Remember, approach this as though you are speaking directly to them. Use 'you', not 'them'.

Outcomes example 1

A sales presentation – pitching your products and services to a new customer.

I want you (the customer) to:

- **Think** that this is the company you want to work with
- **Feel** confident buying from us
- **Say** that you will recommend us as your supplier
- **(Do)** Sign the works order/letter of engagement/ statement of work/purchase order

- **Know** we have your best interests at heart and will deliver

Outcomes example 2

A job interview – why you?

I want you (the interviewers) to:

- **Think** that I am the best candidate for the role

- **Feel** good about supporting my application

- **Say** that I have what you're looking for

- **(Do)** Recommend my application, or better still, hire me

- **Know** that I have the drive to succeed

Outcomes example 3

Introducing change – a new way of working.

I want you (the team) to:

- **Think** this is a good idea, it makes sense to take it on

- **Feel** positive about the proposed new way of working

- **Say** you think it's a great idea and support it publicly

- (**Do**) Agree to try out the new approach straight away

- **Know** that even though we'll face challenges ahead, it will be worth it

Brainstorming

For the next step in the process, stay with your piece of paper or, if you're working as a team, your whiteboard or flip chart. This step can be done almost anywhere and on anything – a daybook, a Post-it note, a reMarkable, Canva, a Teams whiteboard, an old envelope. Some of my clients refer to my method as 'Izzy's back of a cigarette packet' and yes, OK, you could use that if you had to. The point is that you do it; it doesn't matter where.

Consider all the things you could possibly talk about on your topic to your audience to achieve your outcomes. I want you to capture every idea at this stage. Don't try to organise your thoughts or put topics into categories – just brainstorm and capture everything. Your paper (or Post-it note, envelope, whiteboard, flip chart) will look a mess, but that's fine. Keep reminding yourself, 'What are all the things that I *could* talk about on this topic to this audience to achieve those outcomes?'

As you can see in the example below, you now have plenty that you could talk about. It's not arranged in any order, and if you've brainstormed well, there will be too much. Don't worry, that's what we want at this stage.

AUDIENCE: <u>BOARD</u> + <u>CFO</u>

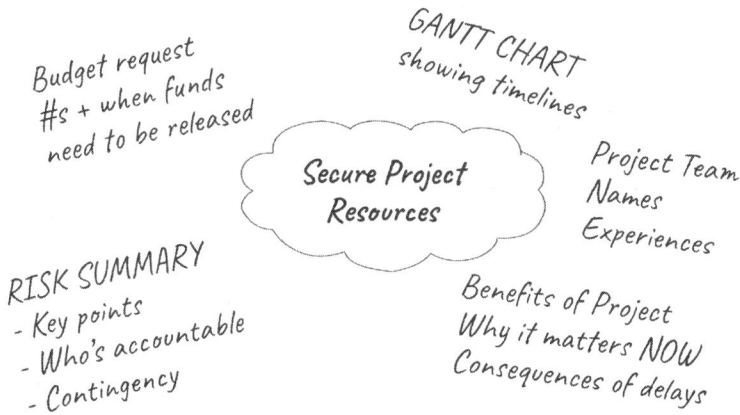

Budget request
#s + when funds
need to be released

GANTT CHART
showing timelines

Secure Project
Resources

Project Team
Names
Experiences

RISK SUMMARY
- Key points
- Who's accountable
- Contingency

Benefits of Project
Why it matters NOW
Consequences of delays

OUTCOME: Think Feel Say Do Know
(transfer from earlier diagram)

When I was at school, my essays always came back with more of my teacher's red ink on than my blue. It must have been depressing for them, and it wasn't great for me, either. Now you can be the teacher and mark your own homework. It's time for you to wield the red pen.

It helps to use a different colour for this. It doesn't have to be red – that's just my throwback to years of returned homework and exam papers, and it makes me feel good to be in charge. It's payback time – and red definitely makes it easier to see what you're doing.

As you edit your own thoughts and ideas, focus on two things:

- The most important points you need to include in your presentation to achieve the outcomes *you* want from *your* audience.

- The fewest number of points you need to cover in your presentation.

Keep asking yourself, 'What *must* I talk about on this topic to this audience to achieve the outcomes (think; feel; say; do; know) I want?'

Why less is more

Imagine the scene – maybe you've been asked to speak for ten minutes or a generous thirty. However long you're speaking for, here's my advice: aim for two, perhaps three, key points. It's a common mistake for presenters to fall into the trap of trying to pack too much in. When you present well, less is more.

The legendary comedian Ken Dodd secured his place in the *Guinness Book of Records* by dishing out over 1,500 jokes in a marathon three-and-a-half hours on stage.[7] Impressive? Yes, but here's the catch – the audi-

---

7   Press Association, 'Master of the marathon show, Sir Ken Dodd once told 1,500 jokes in three-and-a-half hours' (*Mirror*, 12 March 2018), www.mirror.co.uk/3am/celebrity-news/master-marathon-show-sir-ken-12170881, accessed 5 March 2025

ence probably couldn't recall even one of his jokes. Why? Because the more Ken gave, the more they forgot. They were hugely entertained and loved every minute, but their brains couldn't take it all in.

It's the same for us – the more we try to cram into our presentation, the greater the risk that our audience won't just forget some of it, they'll forget the lot.

It's down to a phenomenon known as cognitive load. Picture it as an information traffic jam clogging up our audiences' neural pathways. If we persist in bombarding them, they'll hit cognitive *overload*. The mental circuits seize up – they simply can't process it all – and everything is forgotten in the chaos. It happens with our laptops too. If we overload them and the memory can't handle it, they run slowly, and then seize up.

When you step up to speak or present, don't be a human fire hose. People can't drink from a fire hose, it's too overwhelming. Focus on two or three key points, let them sink in, and enable your audience to retain and remember the valuable items you share. Quality over quantity, every time.

Hence the magic of 5 + or - 2. Most people can remember three things, but nearly everyone can remember two. The French even chunk telephone numbers down into twos – 06 15 95 05 13 – so that they're much easier for recall. Some people will remember five points and a rare few might remember seven. You don't know if your audience is in that rare category (they probably aren't), so it's safer to assume that they're like most of us. Work to the lowest common denominator.

When you stick with a maximum of three key points, you have a good chance that your audience will remember what you said. If you can get it down to two – all the better. You can then make what you say even more memorable, and it will be easier to summarise your key points at the end. We'll get to that later.

Even though you may want to give more – and I really do understand why you feel that way – you are in fact doing your audience a great service by keeping to two or, at the very most, three key points.

Edit, edit, edit

We now focus on the two or three key points that must be at the core of your presentation. Grab your red pen (any other colour will do) or highlighter and simplify what you want to say. This is how you do it most effectively:

- **What's essential?** Which topics stand out as vital to achieving your desired outcomes? These *must* be in your presentation. They are indispensable. Mark them clearly with your pen or highlighter.

- **Connect what matters.** Delve deeper into each key point. Are there sub-points or details that naturally align with the main themes? For instance, if 'Budget' is a key point, consider sub-points such as people costs or resources or materials.

- **Organise with purpose.** Within each key point, organise the associated sub-points with intention. If 'Project Plan' is a key point, bring in your Gantt chart[8] and timelines. This not only clarifies your thinking, it also improves the logic and flow for your audience. Remember, it's not about you, it's about them.

- **Avoid force.** Resist the urge to push elements into points where they don't naturally belong. Step back and be objective – some bits need to stay out. Less is more.

- **Prioritise with purpose.** Continuously ask yourself, 'What *must* I include on this topic to achieve my outcomes, and what *could* I include?' and then prioritise again.

- **Sideline with grace.** Acknowledge that, while there may be valuable information that won't make it into the spotlight this time, it can find its place in future discussions, supplementary materials or a handout. It might come out in your

---

8   Gantt, 'What is a Gantt chart?' www.gantt.com, accessed 6 March 2025

question session after your presentation – it's not wasted, but there isn't room for it right now.

By the end of this process, your presentation should focus on two or three highlighted key points, each supported by relevant sub-points. This strategic organisation not only sharpens your message, it ensures that your audience can easily follow and engage with what you're talking about.

It's hard to be concise. Legend has it that Winston Churchill once wrote to a friend, 'I would have written you a shorter letter, but I didn't have the time.' That's why preparation matters. You owe it to your audience to keep to as few points as possible and to invest the time to prepare.

Let's go back to our Project Resource presentation. What *must* I tell this audience?

I want you (the audience) to:

- **Think** that this is a well-thought-through, well-managed project
- **Feel** confident in me as the project lead
- **Say** that you will approve it
- **(Do)** Release the funds and sign off the budget request

- **Know** we are a strong project team and will deliver on time and on budget

After my brainstorm, I could then chunk down to three key points:

1. A summary of the project showing clearly:
   - How we will deliver on time and on budget
   - How we will manage risk
2. Budget:
   - What needs to be approved, the amount and why
   - When funds need to be released
3. How as a team we will deliver

I'm ready to start drafting my words and considering the supporting materials or slides I might need. I know where I'm going and that what I talk about will achieve the desired outcomes. In the next chapter, I'll show you how you can plan out the whole thing with timings.

How 'think, feel, say, do, know' saved me

One of the things I enjoy immensely in my work is meeting new clients: understanding what challenges they face, what they're trying to achieve, and creating the best training or development programme possible. At those early meetings, I get to know so much and it's a privilege to get close to what's going on.

I was invited to a meeting with a new prospect. I was running a workshop near their offices, so the meeting was arranged for 4.30pm. I could wrap up my session, join my colleague and we'd drive together to meet them.

What could possibly go wrong…?

The first sign of a problem was when, as soon as I got in his car, my colleague asked me, 'Have you got the slide deck, Izzy? I haven't seen it.'

'Slide deck?' I said. 'No, we won't need that. It's an exploratory meeting – we're here to meet the HR director and her team to get a sense of what they want, and for them to hear what you've done on this topic before. We don't need any slides for that.'

'Er, no. There's been a change of plan. Didn't you know? We've been asked to pitch our proposed programme to the HR director and four other board members…'

'*Whaaat*…?' I may have been more colourful in my language. It was a relief I wasn't driving.

Out with my note pad, pencil in hand. Audience at the top – check; outcomes at the bottom (think, feel, say, do, know) – check; topic in the middle – check.

Brainstorm. What *must* I talk about to *this* audience to achieve *those* outcomes? No red pen, but heck, we could still do it. In less than ten minutes, we had a structure and knew where we were going. We were clear on what we could talk about and what key points we wanted to make to achieve the desired outcomes.

I had my opening introduction (more on that later), a story to support our ideas, and we both knew what we would say and what we would do to lead the audience to the desired outcomes (think, feel, say, do, know). What about some slides? Sometimes you're better off without. There was no time to prepare any so I took a gamble.

When we got to the meeting and were settling in and doing our introductions, I said to the board members that I was sure they'd sat through plenty of PowerPoint presentations in the past, so perhaps it would be helpful to do our meeting without any slides and simply bring in some examples of how we would deliver the training. They loved it and we won the project. Phew.

I could never have done it without my 'back of a cigarette packet' method. It saved me and it will save you.

FROM MY HANDS TO YOURS

Mindset

- Recognise that your success as a speaker will come down to how you plan and prepare. Don't be fooled by those 'effortless' speakers able to deliver at the drop of a hat or YouTube videos and influencers who tell you that all you need is a good story. Invest the time to think about your audience and their needs, what outcomes you want to achieve (think, feel, say, do, know) and what you *must* talk about to achieve those outcomes.

Toolset

- Use Audience/Topic/Outcome to position what you're going to talk about so that you connect with what's important to your audience (it's not about you, it's about them).
- Use the radar to understand your audience's needs, results and personal wins.
- Write down what you want your audience to think, feel, say, do, know because of what you talk about.
- Brainstorm everything you could talk about on *your* topic to *your* audience to achieve *your* stated outcomes.
- Keep in mind less is more. Stick to two or three key points, no more.

Have something to write on and something to write with and this method will save you hours.

Skillset

- Identify an upcoming speaking opportunity, the sooner, the better. It doesn't have to be a formal presentation – you might simply be speaking at a meeting or briefing your team. Take your paper (or whatever you choose to use) and write 'audience' at the top, 'topic' in the middle and 'outcomes' at the bottom. Answer all five outcomes. What do you want this audience to go away thinking, feeling, saying, doing or knowing?

In under fifteen minutes, you can create a presentation that speaks directly to your audience and achieves your desired outcomes. With a clear roadmap in hand, you'll be confident to speak without notes, knowing where you're going and what you *must* and *could* include. If you ever find yourself in a tight spot like I did with just minutes to prepare, you can still put together a compelling presentation.

Get ready, you're about to become a presentation powerhouse.

4
My Diamond Is Your New Best Friend

M arilyn Monroe sang that diamonds are a girl's best friend. My diamond is going to be your best friend as a presenter.

The diamond structure will give you your *entire* presentation in one place. Think of it as a satnav guiding you. Your introduction, timings, stories, summary, call to action will all be there. You'll know when to bring in a slide, prop or visual aid; your prompts will be in front of you. You can maintain eye contact with your audience or speak directly to camera if presenting virtually or on video because you'll know what you're going to say and how you're going to make it memorable.

If you choose to use artificial intelligence (AI) to help, that's fine, but do so after you've got your diamond structure. This is where you'll capture your original thoughts – what makes your presentation uniquely *yours*. Best of all, with your diamond, if technology should fail – if your slides don't work, if someone pulls out the cables or the power goes – you can still deliver, without notes, with presence and impact.

That's what will make you a standout speaker.

Know where you're going

Go back to your brainstorm exercise. You are now clear on what you *must* talk about and what you *could* talk about. You have your two or three key points that you're going to include. Remember, more than that and you risk cognitive overload, meaning your audience forgets it all.

The diamond is fatter in the middle than at the top or bottom – this represents the chunky part of your presentation, what I call the 'body', where you'll deliver your key message, whether a pitch, business plan, project update or reasons for being hired. Now it's time to focus on how you top and tail your presentation – how you open, close and restate your call to action. Your diamond structure will make sure you cover all those points – it will be your best friend.

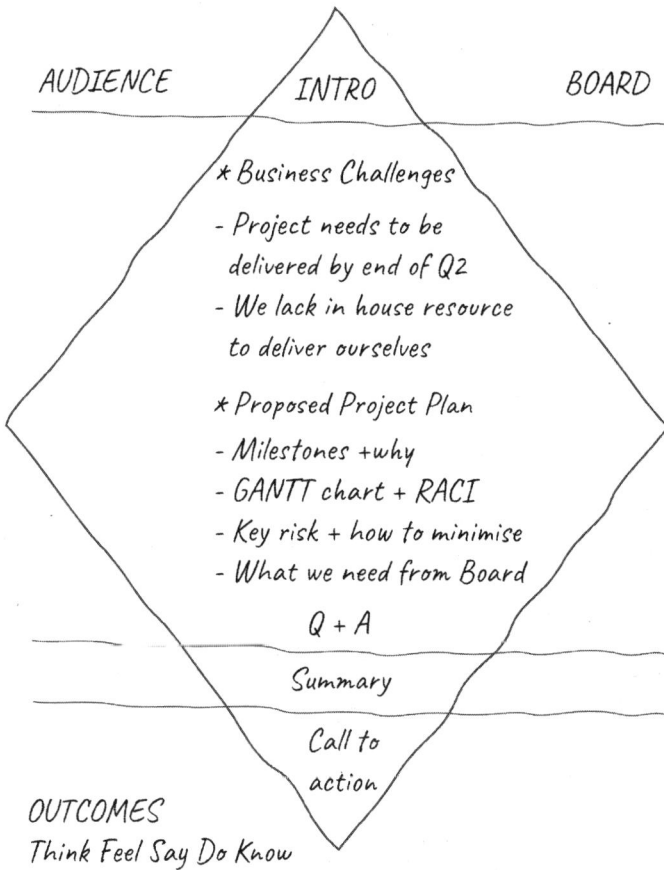

AUDIENCE   INTRO   BOARD

* Business Challenges
- Project needs to be delivered by end of Q2
- We lack in house resource to deliver ourselves

* Proposed Project Plan
- Milestones +why
- GANTT chart + RACI
- Key risk + how to minimise
- What we need from Board

Q + A

Summary

Call to action

OUTCOMES
Think Feel Say Do Know

To help you plan, you can access an interactive PDF of my diamond. Please go to https://masterclass.co.uk/the-diamond. Remember to save it to your system first, then download it to work on it.

Your diamond will be the framework of your presentation from start to finish:

- Your introduction
- The key points and the order you'll make them in
- Your sub-points
- When and where to bring in slides, visual aids or props (note: not every presentation needs a slide deck)
- When to introduce a story
- When to pause
- When to invite questions
- How to summarise
- How to close out with a clear call to action

You'll also have all your timings on your plan as well.

Izzy's diamond, your new best friend.

How to use the diamond

If you brainstorm well when planning, you'll probably have too many points, more than you need for the time available for your presentation. I encouraged you to capture all the things that you could *possibly* talk about on your topic to this audience to achieve your outcomes, and I did that for a reason.

This brainstorming process opens your thinking. You can then step back and, with your audience and outcomes in mind, clarify what you *must* talk about and what you *could* talk about to achieve the outcomes *you* want for *your* audience.

Your sheet of paper (Post-it note, back of the envelope, whiteboard – you choose) is probably very cluttered and looks a mess with things crossed out, red ink, scribbles. It's not currently the best format to help you deliver with impact and presence, but you've got the makings of a great presentation.

Now we transfer your thoughts and ideas on to the diamond.

As you will see, we still have 'Audience' at the top and 'Outcomes' at the bottom. We've also introduced timings down the left-hand side.

Transfer your comments about your audience – what they're like, what's on their radar – to the diamond, and make sure they are easy to read. Now do the same with your outcomes: what you want *your* audience to think, feel, say, do or know. Capture these as though you are talking to your audience, using 'you' not 'them'.

Audience

Introduction

One minute

Body of talk

1. The business case
2. Our proposed solution
(and customer examples to support it)

Three minutes

Four minutes ——————→ Summary

One minute ——————→ Questions and answers

Close &
Call to
action

One minute

Outcomes
THINK, FEEL, SAY, DO, KNOW

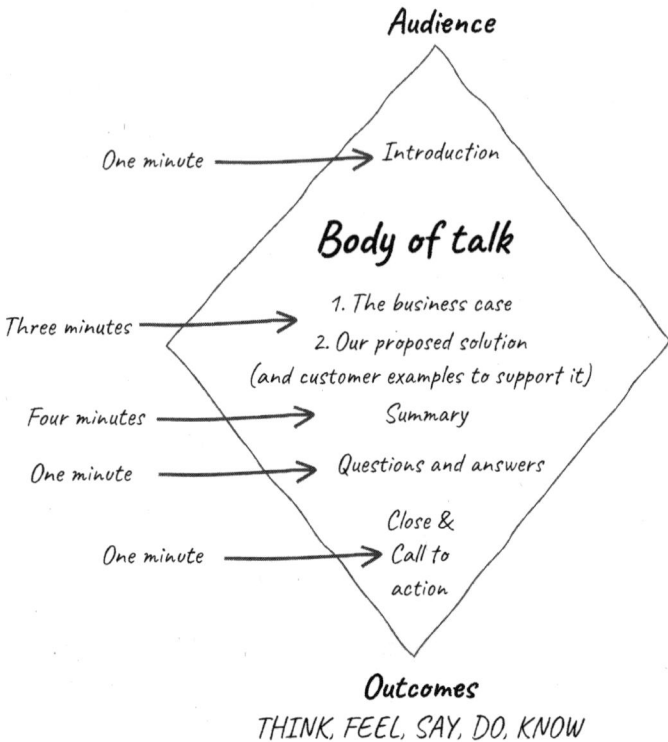

Don't worry if you need to edit or adapt your outcomes at this point. It may take a few iterations. Perhaps it makes sense to swap your points around for them to flow logically. You may focus on a specific outcome – perhaps what you want your audience to *do* or *know*. You can because you now have a clear plan to work from.

As an example, let's look at a presentation for a job interview. Who is the audience? They'll likely be the recruiting director or promotion panel – senior leaders who are looking to see if you are ready to take on this job role or be promoted to the next level. What do you think is on their radar at the moment? What are those big bleeps?

Then, look at outcomes. I want you (the panel) to:

- **Think** that I am the right candidate for this role/promotion

- **Feel** confident in my ability to do this role

- **Say** that you will support my hire/promotion

- **(Do)** Recommend my application

- **Know** that I'm what you're looking for

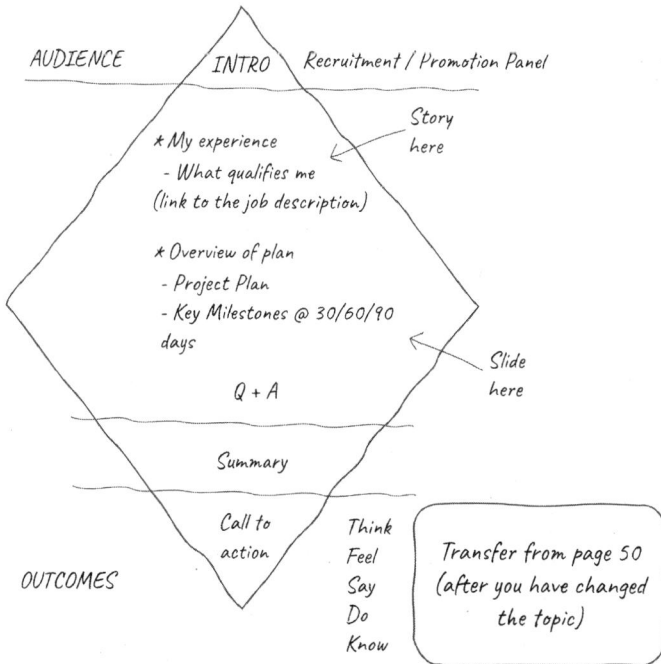

Into the body of your diamond, you now capture the two key points you want to address in this presentation. For example:

- Point 1: Summary of the business challenges.

- Point 2: The proposed project plan.

Or:

- Point 1: My experience and why that makes me qualified for this role.

- Point 2: An overview of my ninety-day plan for when I am appointed/promoted.

We will bring in more detail later.

Why introductions matter

Even if you don't suffer from full-blown glossophobia, you may still get nervous when you come to speak and present. Maybe you get the sweaty palms, the heart palpitations, the dry mouth or worry that you'll forget what you're going to say. This is why you need to plan and prepare the introduction. It's not just to overcome your nerves and settle into your stride, it's for the benefit of your audience.

With your introduction spot on, well-structured and rehearsed, even if you're nervous – and that's

OK – you'll have the impact you need and can lead your audience to the outcomes you want. When we start well, our confidence grows, we get into flow and the nerves fall away. That's why I encourage you to know exactly what you're going to say in your introduction.

Too many presenters, obsessed with the content or the body of their talk, throw away the opportunity to connect with their audience and have impact from the start with their introduction. Think about presentations where you've been in the audience. They may start with 'Hello, my name is... lovely to be with you today...' What a wasted opportunity! Sometimes, the first thing the speaker does is apologise – why do that? – or, ye gods, they read everything from their slides, even their name. Please, no. Some will try a joke, but unless you are an accomplished comedian, can I politely suggest that you don't?

The introduction is your opportunity to create impact with your audience, engage with them, have the presence to hold the room or screen, take them on a great journey and for them to have confidence in you. It's not difficult. It's easy. In fact, it's as easy as ABCD.

This one tool will make a huge difference to your presence and impact as a speaker. It's easy to remember and your confidence will grow every time you use it. An introduction may only last a minute or two, but with ABCD, you will nail your opening.

ABCD stands for:

- **A**ttention – get people listening to you, paying attention to *you*.

- **B**enefits – what's in it for *the audience*? How will they benefit from listening to *you*?

- **C**redentials – your credibility. What qualifies you to speak on this topic today?

- **D**irection – what you'll talk about and how you signpost the way.

Remember this is *just* the introduction, not your actual presentation. Although I will explain each part in detail and give you some examples, your final ABCD introduction should last no more than one or two minutes.

Attention – why does this matter?

Whether you're speaking in person, virtually or at a conference introduced by a moderator, it's likely that your audience will be distracted when you first start. Maybe they're reading emails, checking phones, chatting to colleagues, getting their camera to work, thinking about lunch, or they've just arrived and are settling into their seats. Whatever the situation, you want their full attention on you, not elsewhere.

What are your options? You can say hello or good morning, but if you do, you may waste an opportunity to stand out. Be brave, go for greater impact. Perhaps challenge your audience, make them sit up and really pay attention. For example, open with a statistic, fact or question (it can be rhetorical):

- 'Did you know that over 75% of the population suffer from glossophobia?' and pause.

- 'This project is going to reduce our operating costs by 20% by the end of Q2, a saving of over $250,000,' and pause.

You could open with a story – you'll often see this approach used in TED talks. If you use a story, keep it short and make sure it's relevant to your topic – if it isn't, your audience will spend the rest of the presentation trying to work out why you shared it, not focused on you.

People say a picture paints 1,000 words. Sharing an image and pausing while your audience takes it in can really get their attention. Again, it must be relevant to your topic, and be sure to remember to pause. Give your audience time to take it in.

A technique I call 'What if…?' can be very effective. It works well when you use the question three times, and then follow with 'How does that sound?' For example:

'What if I can show you how to grow our customer base to over 50,000? What if I can show you how we can do that in less than six months? What if we can do that with no increase in marketing spend? How does that sound?' Then look for the nods around the room!

You could simply pause, wait for your audience to settle their attention on you. I've seen people use music, a video clip. There's a great TED talk by Cameron Russell where she changes her clothing on stage – that gets the audience's attention and it's totally relevant to what she goes on to talk about.[9]

This is not the time or place to put in the detail of what you're going to talk about. Use your imagination and make your 'attention' step creative and interesting. You want to have presence and stand out, not be just another speaker.

B – Benefits to your audience

Still tempted to introduce yourself and say who you are? Not yet, hold back. Now's the moment to focus

9   C Russell, 'Looks aren't everything. Believe me, I'm a model' (TEDxMidAtlantic, October 2012), www.ted.com/talks/cameron_russell_looks_aren_t_everything_believe_me_i_m_a_model, accessed 12 March 2025

on your audience and what *they* will gain from listening to you. Remember it's not about you, it's about them. Put yourself in their shoes and ask, as a member of the audience, 'What's in it for me?' Tell them. Be explicit, share what they will gain.

For example:

- 'I'm going to show you how you can nail your introduction every time you present.'
- 'You're going to see how our new campaign will increase online searches by 15%.'
- 'I will explain how we will deliver your project on time and on budget.'
- 'By the end of this session, you'll know what you can do to stand out at your promotion panel and get the offer you want.'

Three things have now happened, very quickly:

1. You've got your audience's attention on you.
2. You've shown how what you'll talk about will benefit *them*. This is why the work you did on your radar in Chapter 2 is so helpful. The more you connect what's in it for them to their big bleeps, the more they pay attention.
3. You've created greater intimacy by using the words 'you' and 'yours'. This brings us back to the Trust Equation, helping your audience feel

that you have their best interests at heart (low self-orientation). Remember, it's not about you, it's about them.

Credentials – why you?

Now it's time to tell the audience about you. The C of your introduction explains what makes you credible. This is your moment to impress and engage them. When you articulate this well, you'll earn what I call the virtual nod – the unspoken acknowledgement from your audience: 'This is good, I'm glad I'm here.'

As you share your credentials, aim to have your audience thinking, 'This speaker clearly knows what they're doing.' It's about instilling confidence that they made the right choice – indeed, a great choice – by attending your presentation (whether they actually had a choice or not).

Here's the twist: stating your credentials may require you to be brave, to step out of your comfort zone and talk about yourself. Embrace this opportunity to showcase your expertise and connect with your audience at a deeper level.

Most people don't like to talk about themselves or to brag about how good, clever or skilled they are, and those that do it too much can be obnoxious. I totally get that, but if you don't tell your audience what qualifies you to speak on this subject today, then who will? If they don't have a sense of why you're the best, most suitable person, why should they listen?

If you are known to them – perhaps you're presenting at a team meeting or a company event – then you don't need to say, 'My name is… and I'm the… at company xxx', but you would at a conference or pitching to a client. Even if your audience knows you well, you still need the C in your ABCD introduction, if just to say why you are speaking today.

For example, 'You all know me. What you might not know is that I've spent the last three months working on a new product that's going to open a huge market for us,' or 'I'm speaking about this project as I've been working on this every day for the last two months. It's one of the most important things we will deliver as a team this year.'

This part of our introduction is key. It is not about creeping death when people introduce themselves and all say pretty much the same: 'Hello, my name is John, I'm a senior manager and I've worked here for six years…' Yawn. If your audience doesn't know who you are, then tell them, but remember they need to know three things: your name, what you do and what qualifies you to speak on this topic today.

For example, 'My name's Isobel Rimmer, I'm founder of Masterclass Training and a presentation skills coach.

I've trained hundreds of business leaders and pre-pared well-known politicians to present with impact on TV and radio, and I'm a regular contributor on Sky News on the topic of personal image and impact.'

It's OK to brag a little bit, even if that feels uncom-fortable. This is about what makes you credible as a speaker. It isn't for your benefit, it's for the audience, so they can see why you're qualified to speak on this topic and why they should listen.

I know the sequence may feel strange at first, but if you still have a strong desire to state who you are up front, believe me, the audience won't be listening. They're not ready to hear it, and so they'll miss it. Get their atten-tion (A), share the benefits and what's in it for them (B), and then come in with your credentials (C) to tell them why you're qualified to talk about this topic today.

D - Direction

Your audience needs to know where you're going, the direction your presentation will take and what's expected of them. In the same way that a newsreader shares the headlines first before they go into the detail, you use the D of your introduction to signpost the way for the *benefit of your audience*.

Most audiences don't know what you want them to do. Are they supposed to ask questions, and if so, when? Do they need to take notes, will there be handouts or copies of slides? How long will this presentation take? Are they expected to vote at the end or take some action? Will coffee be available?

When you signpost the way for your audience, you give them a heads up to what's coming and make it easier for them to retain your key points. They relax because now they know what they're supposed to do.

The final part of your D will turbo charge your introduction. Signpost what you're going to talk about, and then use the phrase 'so that' to link directly to the outcomes you captured: what you want your audience to think, feel, say, do or know.

For example:

- 'Over the next fifteen minutes, I'm going to talk about x, y and z *so that* you can be confident in our project plan, know that we will deliver on time and on budget, release the budget and make sure any questions you have are answered.'

- 'In the hour we have together, I'm going to share the research updates and production schedules *so that* you know exactly when the new products will be available and can confidently plan your distribution schedules for Q1 and Q2 with our channel partners.'

- 'Over the next ten minutes, I will share my plan for the first ninety days in this new role *so that* you can see how I can make a difference from the outset, you can have confidence in me as your preferred candidate and be comfortable recommending my application.'

As you bring the ABCD together, see how it looks:

- **A**: 'Over 75% of people suffer from glossophobia – a fear of public speaking.' Pause.

- **B**: 'If you get even slightly anxious when you speak or present, this session is for you. I'm going to show you how you can create a powerful introduction that will help you nail every presentation, face to face or online.'

- **C**: 'My name's Isobel Rimmer, founder of Masterclass Training. I've coached hundreds of business leaders and well-known politicians to present with impact on TV, and I'm a regular contributor on Sky News as a presentation skills pundit.'

- **D**: 'Over the next fifteen minutes, I'll show you how to build your introduction using my ABCD tool *so that* whenever you present, you will engage with your audience, be confident in your message, share what makes you the expert, have presence. Not only will you know exactly where you're going, but your audience will, too.'

(Out loud, timed at fifty-one seconds.)

Putting the meat on the bones

Let's now go back to the body of our presentation and, using our example of requesting funds for a project plan, put some meat on the bones.

We identified two key points that *must* be shared:

1. A summary of the business challenges (to demonstrate we understand the audience's need).

2. The proposed project plan (to show we know what we're doing).

We transfer the *key* points we want to make from our brainstorm sheet. For example:

- **Business challenges**: Lack of resource on project x; quicker turnaround required to meet funding deadlines.

- **Proposed project plan**: Key milestones, a Gantt chart, risk review, sign off and completion dates. We might include a responsible, accountable, consult, inform (RACI) chart for this audience.

When coaching presenters, I find this is the area that people are least concerned about. They know their topic. They should! The challenges are:

- Keeping content tight – stick to two or three key points

- Getting a logical flow – to make the presentation easier for the audience to follow

- Making key points memorable – they must stick

- When and where to use slides and visual aids

FROM MY HANDS TO YOURS

Mindset

- Great presenters connect with what matters to their audience – it's not about you, it's about them. Take them on a journey, being clear on what the outcomes are (what you want them to think, feel, say, do or know).

- Get in the mindset of your audience – see things from their perspective.

- Recognise that success comes as much from your preparation as your delivery. The investment you make in preparation is key to being a great speaker.

Toolset

- Prepare and brainstorm using Topic, Audience and Outcomes. Be clear what you want your audience to think, feel, say, do or know, and write it down.

- Brainstorm all the things you could possibly speak about on this topic to this audience to achieve these outcomes.

- Edit and pare back. What *must* you talk about on this topic to this audience to achieve these outcomes, and what *could* you talk about? Distil back to two or three key points, no more.

- My diamond is your best friend. Use it to frame up your presentation, transferring your brainstorm ideas and content across. Remember the key points – two or possibly three, no more – that you will talk about go in the body of your presentation.

- Download the diamond PDF https://masterclass. co.uk/the-diamond so that you can use it quickly and easily. Remember to save it to your system before using it.

- Use ABCD (attention, benefits, credentials, direction) to prepare what you will say in your introduction. It may only be a few minutes, but the introduction sets you up, takes away your nerves and engages your audience. Not only will you know where you're going, so will your audience.

Skillset

- Take every opportunity to practise using the diamond. It doesn't have to be a full-blown presentation – you might be holding a team update. The more you use it, the more comfortable you become and the quicker you can transfer your ideas into a coherent presentation that flows.

- Write down your ABCD introduction and practise out loud so that you know exactly what you're going to say. Rehearse and remember to pause – allow time for your audience to catch up and what you say to sink in.

- Time your introduction – one or two minutes maximum.

- Experiment using different ways to capture your topic, audience and outcomes. You might find an

A4 sheet of paper is best, or a notebook, or Post-it notes. I use a reMarkable.

You may be tempted to leap into AI, but before you do your prompts, be clear on your topic, who your audience is and what outcomes you want to achieve. AI can then help you know *what* you're talking about, *who* you're talking to and *what* you want them to go away thinking, feeling, saying, doing or knowing.

PART TWO

DELIVER WITH IMPACT – LET'S TALK ABOUT YOU

When I train and coach presenters, I find it best to split sessions into two parts – firstly, how to *prepare* for impact, and secondly, how to *deliver* with impact.

Having a great structure, logical flow and relevant content is essential, but it is wasted if your delivery doesn't excite or engage your audience. Equally, it doesn't matter how much charisma and presence you have if your content is poorly structured and all over the place.

The great speakers, those who stand out and we remember, give their full attention to both preparation *and* delivery.

5

Breaking Through The Anxiety And Worry

The idea of standing up and speaking to an audience, going live on TV, presenting at a promotion panel or job interview can fill us with horror. It's glossophobia taking over.

To understand what's going on, we need to go back in our evolution and explore a part of our brain called the amygdala. This small almond-shaped cluster of nuclei plays a crucial role in the processing of emotions, particularly those related to fear and pleasure, and it's got a lot to answer for. When it comes to presenting and why we get nervous, there are three things that our amygdala does to cause all sorts of problems:

Emotional processing. It's there to protect us from danger, so it helps in the rapid processing and recognition of emotions, particularly fear. If we are frightened or scared, it watches out for us like a guardian angel.

Forming memories. It is involved in the consolidation of memories, especially those associated with emotional experiences – good and bad. If you've had a negative experience (a presentation that went wrong or where you froze and couldn't remember what to say), the amygdala reminds you what happened and, because it's looking to protect you, convinces you that experience is best avoided. It really is trying to help – even if it doesn't feel like it at the time.

Fight, flight or freeze. It's a key player in the body's response to stress and threat, and can trigger the fight, flight or freeze response by activating the sympathetic nervous system to release adrenaline, putting us on high alert. This leads to physiological changes such as increased heart rate, heightened senses and the release of stress hormones.

When your heart is pounding, you feel a red flush spreading across your chest and your voice wobbles, thank your amygdala. It's trying to protect and save you from danger.

The fight, flight or freeze response is particularly important. Our amygdala is telling us that when we present to an audience, it's dangerous and risky. Go back thousands of years, if twenty pairs of eyes are on you, they're probably hostile. Maybe a tribe of warriors is coming to kill you, armed with spears, or a pack of wolves is eying you up for dinner. Your brain is telling you to run away (flight), get ready to stand up to them (fight) or stay very still (freeze) so they won't see you. They'll walk on by, put away their spears and leave you alone.

The physiological changes – the increased heart rate, the heightened senses – are due to the hormone adrenaline pumping round your body, giving you the energy in your legs and extremities to get the hell out of there. Meanwhile, the stress hormone, cortisol, is increasing blood sugar levels, giving you a super quick energy source when things get stressful. It's Formula One fuel to help you escape.

If you're going to run the 100 metres in the Olympic Games or play ninety minutes of football, then you want adrenaline and cortisol to make you go faster and react quicker, but if you're about to deliver a winning pitch to the board of directors and come across as composed, confident and competent, you've got to do something to counteract their effects.

How can we use nerves to our advantage?

Let's look at these challenges from a different perspective. We do want adrenaline and cortisol, just not too much. Those hormones help us perform at our best, give an edge to our presentation, carry us through, but we need to tip the balance so they don't spoil our delivery.

The secret? Retain some of the adrenaline and cortisol, but get rid of the excess. If you have no nerves, your delivery will lack energy; too many and you're all over the place.

My first recommendation is to focus on relabelling. Instead of feeling the emotion and calling it 'nervous', feel it and relabel it with a more positive word – 'excited', for example. When you're excited, you're motivated and you feel good. 'I'm *excited* about delivering this presentation. I'm *excited* about speaking live on TV or radio. I'm *excited* about the opportunity to meet the board of directors. I'm *excited* at the opportunity to interview for this job.' See the difference?

People tend to underestimate the power of relabelling. Work with it, try it and you'll see how it can help change your perspective. Stick with it. You can't relabel once and think that's enough; remind yourself to do it regularly until it becomes part of what you do, and you'll find that you start to shake off those negative thoughts and feelings.

While you help your brain to relabel, there are physical things that you can do, too. Power poses are a good example.

There's a great TED talk by social psychologist Amy Cuddy viewed by millions of people.[10] In it, she speaks about how to fake it till you make it and fake it till you are it. Some people question her research, but I know from my own experience of using her power poses that they work for me. I certainly feel more confident, in control and ready to present afterwards, and I've had the same feedback from people I've coached. It will do you no harm, so why not give power poses a go yourself?

Amy's power poses are physical positions, stances that you hold for two minutes before you present or go into a high-stakes situation such as an interview. There are four that I recommend. I've used them all with positive results.

1. **Wonder Woman** – Hands on hips, feet apart – wider than your hips. Stand straight, survey all around you, grow tall through your spine, chest out. You can practise breathing exercises and voice warm-ups at the same time. You don't need to dress like Wonder Woman, nor have her incredible legs. I certainly don't.

2. **The Winner** – The position we adopt when we win a race. Arms straight up above you, head thrown slightly back, feet apart – think

---

10 A Cuddy, 'Your body language may shape who you are', (TEDGlobal, June 2012), www.ted.com/talks/amy_cuddy_your_ body_language_may_shape_who_you_are

Usain Bolt in the Olympics. You've won – the excitement! Hold it for two minutes.

3. If you want a seated option, try my **Dominant Executive** where you lean back in your chair, hands behind your neck, elbows out to the side, one leg crossed over the other with the upper knee out to the side, looking down your nose. It's a position that shows no fear, exposes the soft underbelly and commands space. Imagine the CEO of an organisation doing it from a large executive chair in the boardroom. (Note: this is not one to do in public if you're wearing a skirt or a kilt.)

4. **Leaning In** – This fourth one is quite subtle. Stand behind a chair and put both hands on the back rest – as though you're going to push the chair into its place. Straighten your arms and extend one leg behind you, stretching out your calf muscles. Hold that position for two minutes. Most people will have no idea that what you're doing is a power pose – it looks just like a stretch.

A two-minute power pose can result in you reducing the levels of cortisol, the stress hormone, and boosting testosterone, making you feel stronger and more in control. According to Amy Cuddy, the benefits can last for up to twenty minutes – long enough for most presentations and certainly to get into your stride and deliver a great introduction.

Managing nerves without anyone knowing

You may be feeling relaxed and confident, and then suddenly, an adrenaline rush is upon you. If you're in the board room or on a Teams call, or on stage or in the studio, it simply isn't possible to use a power pose, but you need to do something as you feel that anxiety flood over you.

This is where your presentation toolset comes into its own with techniques you can do without anyone knowing. Conscious breathing is one of them. Later I'll talk more about how you can use different breathing exercises to give your voice greater resonance and depth, but for now, I want to concentrate on what to do in the moment when adrenaline kicks in, you feel anxiety and you want the floor to swallow you up.

My go-to technique is 4 × 4 breathing. I learned it from a TV producer on Sky News, and I've used it and coached others on it thousands of times since. It's also known as box breathing and is recommended by the US Navy SEALs to handle stress, so you're in good company with this one.

Before you start, exhale through your mouth to empty your lungs. Then, calmly:

1. Inhale through your nose for a count of four

2. Hold your breath for a count of four

3. Exhale through your mouth for a count of four

4. Hold your breath for a count of four

Repeat several times. I find three or four rounds is enough to calm me, but even just one round of 4 × 4 will reduce anxiety and clear your mind.

If you've never done this before, here are some tips to get you started:

- Find a quiet space where you won't be disturbed. I suggest you sit upright on a chair for the first few times. It can also help to close your eyes so you can concentrate purely on your breathing.

- Place one hand on your chest and the other hand on your stomach, and feel where the breath comes in and leaves. If you're breathing deeply, you can feel your diaphragm move in and out.

Now let's return to that boardroom meeting or Teams call. Clearly you can't disappear off into some Zen state and close your eyes with a panel in front of you or cameras running, but you can do 4 × 4 breathing quietly and gently, and no one need know. Your lips will barely move and even a close-up camera won't pick up what you're doing.

As you get more skilled and confident in 4 × 4, increase the count – taking it up to 4 × 5 or 4 × 6. Breathe in for five, hold for five, breathe out for five and hold for five. There are some people who are comfortable taking it up to 4 × 10. That may be OK if you're preparing in the background, but not if you're live; you may faint.

Another good exercise is 4–7–8. Here, the calmness is obtained by breathing out for longer than you breathe in:

- Inhale through your nose for a count of four.
- Hold your breath for a count of seven.
- Exhale through your mouth for a count of eight.

In out, in out, shake it all about

If you watch a football or rugby game, you'll notice this when a player is substituted. The player about to come on will have warmed up (of course, and so should we when we present – more on that later), but as they take their final instructions from the coach, notice how they're jumping around – hopping from foot to foot, tugging at their clothes. That's adrenaline in action. They need those hormones pumping to be ready to run and play at their best, but unconsciously, they're getting rid of the excess through their movement.

When you present, you too need to get rid of the excess adrenaline so that you have enough to give your presentation the sparkle but not come across as manic.

One of the most effective ways is to simply shake it out through your hands and feet. Not always possible if you're on stage or in the boardroom, but if you're on a Zoom call, take yourself off camera and do your shake outs.

Be careful that you have space to do this – you don't want to bruise your arms or break any furniture. Start with your hands – shake each one out as though you're trying to rid them of lots of water. Do it several times. Now your feet – imagine something unspeakable is stuck to the bottom of your shoe and you're trying to get rid of it. Shake out each foot as hard as you can. Then do hands and feet together – not both feet at the same time, obviously.

This gets rid of the excess adrenaline. When you're done, just rest your hands by your sides and stand with your feet hip width apart. You may feel a tingle in the extremities, but you'll also feel a sense of calm. You're ready to perform.

You may not be able to do this whenever you're about to present, but if you are near a bathroom, just pop in, wash your hands, and then shake them out vigorously. Absolutely no one will know (unless they've read it here) that what you're doing is getting rid of your nerves.

You can practise anywhere, anytime

We often assume that the people we see on television – newsreaders, pundits, politicians, speakers in the public eye – have no fear of presenting. That's simply not true.

I was asked to coach a UK member of parliament who would be taking part in a series of radio interviews and was lined up for *Question Time* on TV. This is a programme where a live studio audience poses questions to a panel, none of whom have seen the questions beforehand.

She is a good speaker – eloquent, passionate about her politics and enthusiastic. I didn't want to lose any of those strengths, so we focused on three things – power poses, relabelling her fears and breathing.

I encouraged her to practise 4 × 4 breathing wherever she could – for example, in a taxi to the radio studio; on the train when going to her constituency. If she had the time and space, she could stretch it out, pushing up to 4 × 5 or 4 × 6, but if she only had a few moments, she could still get the results. Every day, she practised 4 × 4.

She also worked on relabelling her emotions. She did it before she went to bed, in the shower, before meetings until it became part of her daily routine. She developed her own power poses that she used for two minutes – some obvious, some subtle.

It worked. On reviewing the recording of *Question Time* and how she came across on the radio, she couldn't believe how much better she looked and sounded. Not only did she deliver her interviews and handle her questions very well, she shifted from feeling nervous and uncomfortable about doing this to enjoying it. She pushed the boundaries and found a new energy and strength. Yes, she still gets nervous, but she channels that energy positively and gets rid of the excess.

Power poses, relabelling and breathing made all the difference to this politician. They can work for you, too.

You can also use these techniques in other stressful situations. A few years ago, I suffered a detached retina, losing the vision in my left eye – it was pretty scary. I ended up at Moorfields in London where a brilliant surgeon sorted it.

I went in assuming (wrongly) that I would have a general anaesthetic. The idea of being awake with just a local anaesthetic to numb the pain was worse than all the boardroom pitches I've ever done. I was, frankly, terrified.

I didn't have a choice; I just had to trust my surgeon and my own techniques for handling nerves. As soon as he started the procedure, I began 4 × 4 breathing. I focused on inhaling, counting, exhaling, counting, and repeated it over and over. I became almost trance like and completely relaxed.

The surgery wasn't in any way painful – the local anaesthetic worked, although the sensation was a bit weird. When all was done and the nurse was patching up my eye, the surgeon kindly said what a good patient I'd been – I bet he says that to everyone – and how I hadn't moved an inch, which had made his job easier. I explained what I'd done and how I'd used 4 × 4 breathing to help me stay calm. He'd never heard of it, and I ended up coaching the scrub nurses and the theatre team as well as the surgeon. He now recommends 4 × 4 to all his patients – to his benefit and theirs.

We often feel that we're the only one who's nervous, anxious and suffering the sweaty palms. We look around and everyone else seems confident, calm and composed.

Don't be fooled. Most people are anxious, many very anxious indeed, and we all need some adrenaline coursing through our veins. It gives us the energy to perform at our best. The secret is to get rid of the excess.

Those who have managed to get that balance of energy and confidence have learned how to do it. They've applied their breathing techniques, they've discovered ways to relabel their emotions, they're probably all using some kind of power pose and they've rehearsed again and again until they feel in control.

As one of my colleagues says, 'Tomorrow is the first day of the rest of your life.' Like my politician, find opportunities every day to put into practice what I've shared with you here. Do this and you'll see why Amy Cuddy says in her TED talk that you can fake it not just until you make it, but until you *become* it.

FROM MY HANDS TO YOURS

Mindset

- Recognise that it's OK to be nervous. It's a natural state and it's one you want to have. Without adrenaline and a few nerves, your delivery will lack energy. The secret is to make sure you don't have too much and to get rid of the excess. Rather than try to get rid of it all, embrace it. Celebrate the fact that adrenaline will make you a better speaker and enhance your delivery.

- Relabel how you feel about presenting. Instead of it being nerve wracking, relabel your mindset as 'exciting' or 'fun' or 'motivating'. This idea of reframing your mindset is more powerful than you can possibly imagine.

Toolset

- Practise your 4 × 4 breathing in as many different situations as you can. Get to the point where you can simply slip into 4 × 4 and calm yourself. It even works during root canal.

- If time is limited, simply find an opportunity to breathe in and then breathe out for longer. Use your

4-7-8 technique. In for four seconds, hold for seven seconds, out for eight seconds. No one will know.

- Try a variety of different power poses and hold them for two minutes.

Skillset

- Remember a skill is a technique you can use under pressure. The more you practise your breathing in a safe environment when you're *not* nervous, the more confident you get in relabelling how you feel when anxiety creeps up on you, the more frequently you practise your exercises to reduce the adrenaline and boost your testosterone, the easier it will become.

6
Looking Good, Feeling Good

'Looking good, Billy-Ray.'

'Feeling good, Lewis.'

These iconic lines from the film *Trading Places* capture a moment of triumph. As the characters, played by Eddie Murphy and Dan Aykroyd, soak up the sun in the Caribbean, they embody success, confidence and the joy of accomplishment. Looking good and feeling good go hand in hand.

In your journey to become a great presenter, it's essential to remember that while the focus should be on your audience, your appearance and self-assurance play a significant role in how your message is received. I've repeatedly said that it's not about you, it's about them, but we can't ignore that you are on display, and to perform at your best, you need to look good and feel good, too. When you look good and feel good, your inner confidence radiates to your audience.

In this chapter, we'll explore practical strategies to ensure you look your best, especially in today's virtual world. It's not just about aesthetics; it's about the powerful connection between appearance and confidence.

A close friend of mine – a brilliant presenter, trainer and coach – once shared with me her secret for presentation success. 'Izzy, I always wear my best and most beautiful underwear when doing an important presentation or speaking at a conference. Only I know, but it makes me feel good, and if I feel good, I know I look good, and if I look good, I present better.'

Great advice. Sort out that underwear drawer.

Why posture matters

Think about what happens to our posture when we're nervous or anxious. We hunch our shoulders, bring our elbows into our sides, perhaps fold our arms, lower our head slightly, cast our eyes down. Women often cross their legs when standing – mad really as it makes them wobble, especially if they're wearing high heels. Some people might turn sideways to take up less space.

What we're doing is making ourselves smaller, less significant to our audience. That sneaky amygdala is at work again, protecting us by making us a difficult target, harder for those warriors to get us with their spears or the wolves to eat us for breakfast. It goes against all logic and reason to stand tall – take our elbows out to the side and step into the space available. Why put ourselves at risk?

When we present, whether we're standing or seated, posture matters. Good posture makes us look taller and more confident. We associate success with height and stance. US presidential election results show that the taller candidate nearly always wins.[11] A coincidence?

Try following these seven steps. They will help you have greater presence:

1. Stand with your feet hip-width apart. When nervous, women tend to bring their feet closer together, while men often take up what I call the 'John Wayne' with their feet spaced wider than their hips. Stick to hip width (and no, madam, your hips are *not* that big) to help you be grounded.

---

11 D Maclean, 'Americans tend to elect the tallest person for president – here's how the 2020 candidates would fare' (*Independent*, 18 November 2019), www.independent.co.uk/news/world/americas/us-politics/us-election-tallest-candidates-trump-height-biden-warren-obama-a9207876.html, accessed 7 March 2025

2. Position your feet at five to one (like the hands of a clock) slightly turned out. This will give you core stability and you won't wobble, even if you're nervous. Avoid locking your knees – it's bad for them and will make you rigid. Relax. Keep your weight slightly on the balls of your feet, not your heels.

3. Very gently tighten the muscles in your buttocks (don't clench them – a gentle squeeze is all you need). You will feel two things, both positive: your bottom will come underneath you and your tummy will tuck in, making you look taller and slimmer.

4. Before you do anything else, try slumping while holding this position. You can't. Relax your buttocks and you'll find you can slump. Good posture means no slumping. Repeat Step 3 before you move to Step 5.

5. Imagine your spine is like a series of cotton reels, a thread running up through the middle. Someone is gently pulling you up by the thread. Grow tall through your spine, keeping your shoulders relaxed and down. If you're doing this in front of a mirror, you'll see how beautiful and elegant your posture is now. No mirror? Just feel the elegance, luxuriate in it.

6. Take your elbows out to the side and create a little gap under your armpits. This gives you an inverted triangle shape with your body and

makes you look more confident (we tend to jam our elbows into our sides when we're nervous).

7. Bring your hands together as though you are about to clap and rest them gently in front of you (keep that gap under your armpits). Alternatively, rest your left hand on top of your right hand with your right thumb touching your third (ring) finger on your left hand. If you wear a ring, lightly touch it. Don't clasp your fingers – you're not praying – and don't fiddle with your rings – that's adrenaline kicking in.

I recommend this last point to position your hands. It works with the good posture you now have, and if you are holding notes or a microphone or a slide clicker, it's a natural position. It's also a great hand position from which you can gesture outwards.

As you become more confident, you will find it easier to stand with your hands by your sides, but for now, give them something to do by letting them rest gently in front of you. Keep your hands around waist height; don't drop them down to what I call the 'fig leaf' protecting the crown jewels. You're not defending a free kick.

If you're seated at a panel meeting, in a boardroom or on a virtual call, try these techniques to have great posture, presence and gravitas:

- **Bottom to back of chair (BBC).** This is one of my favourites. Look at any newsreader, TV pundit or presenter and you will see they have their bottom firmly in the back of their chair. They're taught to do this.

  Think about it – if you're nervous, where will you sit? On the edge of your chair! Why? So that you can make your escape (flight) – your amygdala is protecting you again. If you sit with your bottom on the edge of your seat, when you start to relax, you'll end up slumping back and that's not a good look. With BBC, you can relax back and stay upright, and you can move forward, all the time maintaining great posture and presence.

- **Feet flat on floor (FFOF).** Make sure that your seat is positioned so that you can have your bottom as far back as possible (BBC) while keeping your FFOF. Don't sit so far back that your legs are dangling – adjust the seat if you can. Don't cross your legs – if you need some modesty, tuck your feet slightly to one side. FFOF will help your core and stability, just as your five to one position with your feet helps you when you're standing.

- Take your elbows out to the side and create a little gap under your armpits as you did when standing.

- Place your wrists on the table in front of you (if there is one) to make sure your hands are in sight. You risk looking shifty if your hands aren't visible.

- Draw yourself up through your spine (as before, think of those cotton reels and a thread running up the middle). Lean slightly forward and, if on camera (Teams, Zoom etc), look straight at it and smile. If you are in a room, perhaps a boardroom or with a panel of people in front of you, sweep your eyes round, not too quickly, make eye contact with every person present and smile.

If you want to have more impact, arrive after your audience is seated. This may not always be possible but if you are presenting in person, practise your stance, and then walk confidently to your speaking position taking the longer route and 'owning' the room.

There are a few things you should notice.

You walk more slowly because you're concentrating on your posture and gently tucking your buttocks underneath you, so you will appear more in control, and this gives you greater presence. People who are confident don't scamper or fidget. Did you ever see Queen Elizabeth run? People were more likely to run after her. Adrenaline and nerves speed us up – when we slow down, we have more presence.

Your arms and gestures are more open. You expose the 'target' (the soft underbelly) because you now have no fear of the spears of the warriors or the hunger of the wolves. Your confidence makes other people feel confident in what you have to say. You're inviting people into your space.

Take your hands out and towards your audience, keeping your palms and thumbs upwards. In doing so, you take up more space. Confident people naturally take up space; indeed, we give people with authority more space as a sign of respect. The more space you take up, the more presence you will have. Just don't invade other people's space.

With good posture and open gestures, you'll find yourself looking around more (not looking down at your feet or avoiding eye contact), which further increases your presence and makes you more engaging too. However, maintaining eye contact with your audience can be hard. Do it too well and you may lose your train of thought. If you are in a room of between four and twelve people, I recommend you focus on an imaginary dot between their eyebrows as opposed to looking directly into their eyes. This allows you to give the impression of eye contact without losing your concentration, but don't do this in a one to one or small group setting – you will look squiffy.

If you are presenting in a theatre-style set-up looking out to the audience, draw an imaginary figure five with them. Start top right, slowly move your eye contact across the back rows, down and round through the middle, and finish your five bottom left before gradually taking your eye contact back up to top right. This will give the audience the impression that you are looking at everyone, even if under the lights you can't see them properly.

Laugh and the world laughs with you

Let's look at what happens to facial expressions when we're nervous. One of two things is likely – neither of which boosts presence and impact.

Firstly, many people smile more when they're nervous. I find this is often the case for women. If we smile too much, we can look needy, anxious and desperate to please.

Other people smile less when they're nervous. They may grimace or clench their teeth. I find men are more prone to this. They then come across as uncomfortable, disinterested, grim, angry even.

How do you get it right?

Make sure that your head is upright – not tipped back and not looking down. Try this: drop your head with your chin touching your chest, your eyes looking into your lap. Now smile with your head in that position.

It's hard work – you've really got to force those muscles. Bring your head back to the vertical position and smile – how much easier is it now? You're not fighting gravity so can break into a natural smile.

Remember, don't smile too much. Just look as though you could smile easily and naturally.

What to wear

Entire books are dedicated to what to wear, and TikTok and YouTube are full of videos about choosing colours. I trained as a Colour Me Beautiful[12] consultant many years ago, precisely to help people look their best when presenting. Here are my three aspects to focus on, whether you're speaking in person or on camera:

1. Colours

2. Structure and shape

3. Pattern

At a colour consultation, you will discover which colours look best against your skin tone, eye colour and suit your personal style. It's done by draping different coloured fabrics against your face and seeing which ones make you look more vibrant or tired. You

---

12 Colour Me Beautiful home page, www.colourmebeautiful.co.uk, accessed 6 March 2025

will know exactly what works best for you, it will be easier to choose the right clothing, and you won't need as many outfits. You'll discover which shade of red or blue brings out the best in you and whether a soft cream or a pure white works against your complexion.

When you're presenting virtually, choose a block colour. You might love a white shirt or prefer to stick with blacks and greys, but a brighter block colour will have more impact on camera. Go for contrast between a shirt/blouse and your jacket – for example, a warm-tone red jacket over a cream or beige dress. Women often default to wearing black – it's easy, but it is a harsh colour and can make you look tired.

For men, choosing the best shirt colour matters because it is right next to your face. A strong or deep blue will look fantastic on some, but show up a five o'clock shadow on others. Pink and lilac can work brilliantly for many, even though some men wouldn't naturally choose them.

When we present, we want to draw attention to our face. We look to clothing to create a clear outline that gives structure to our shoulders and comes in at the waist. Work with your body shape – be that straight, round, pear or apple – not against it. If in doubt, always opt for elegantly loose rather than anything tight. Even the best presenters are let down if their shirt buttons are straining or, worse, flesh is on show.

When you're presenting in person, think about where you'll stand and how you'll move. For women presenting on stage, keep heels low to make it easier to move around. Even if you're comfortable in high heels, nerves will make you less stable (you may cross your legs and wobble). Better not to take the risk.

Your backdrop matters. Hours are spent on political campaigns making sure that the candidates' clothes look good against the party colours. You might be using a company colour or logo on Teams – check in advance that what you're wearing contrasts well.

Block colours are a safer bet than stripes, squares or patterns. Checks can strobe under studio lighting and distract your audience. If you're filming in a studio, ask if there will be a green screen and get advice on what colours to avoid. If in doubt, take two outfits – better to be prepared. You don't want to disappear into the green.

A pop of colour is a quick and easy way to add interest and energy. For men, that might be their shirt or a brightly coloured tie. For women, a scarf or a block-coloured top.

Think ahead – if you're on TV or using a mic (lapel or other), then accessories may cause a problem. I remember listening to a famous divorce lawyer I know being interviewed on national radio and hearing a strange rattle throughout. It turned out it was her necklace – a beautiful piece, I've seen her wear it many times, but it was knocking against her mic, and so distracted me from what she was saying.

If you suspect that you might fiddle when you get nervous – with your ring, hair, watch, cufflinks, necklace – remove those items. OK, not your hair, but perhaps tie it up or back.

Lighting and make-up

It comes to us all.

I was filming a series of training videos, and my producer was an experienced BBC executive. After a few takes, I had to face reality – I didn't like what I was seeing on the screen. I am realistic, I'm no beauty, but I asked what I could do to look better. He gently told me that as we get older, there are two things to consider. The first is lighting. The second? Acceptance.

He was right. We changed the lighting, and I did look better. I'm coming to terms with the second...

Given there's not much I can do about the way I look (I blame my parents and a swimming race when I broke my nose), I now appreciate the importance of good lighting. You should too. It will make a big difference to every virtual presentation.

In a TV studio, there should be professionals there to ensure the lighting is optimal. All you do is take up the offer of make-up and hair. Don't be macho about it (whatever your age or sex). Accept that everyone looks better with make-up under studio lighting and the professional artists know what they're doing. It's their job. Trust them, however uncomfortable you might feel about having powder on your bald patch.

The first time I did TV work, I was horrified at how much make-up the artists used and how 'big' my hair was (a heck of a lot of hair spray), but it looked fine on the playback. I only realised just how much make-up I had on when looking in the car's rear-view mirror and nearly reversed into a bollard.

I've coached many leaders and politicians who insist that it's what they have to say that matters, not how they look. I've trained young entrepreneurs who argue that if Richard Branson can get away with a pullover or Steve Jobs a black T shirt, then why can't they? I know – it shouldn't matter, but it does. People will judge you, perhaps unfairly, in the first few seconds. They'll make up their minds about your ability based on the cut of your trousers before the interview begins, so why fight it? When you are as successful as Branson, you can do what you want, too.

A friend of mine, a former air stewardess, talks of the importance of her 'landing lipstick' – a quick pop of colour and gloss as the crew prepares for landing. We should always aim to look our best, not just for us, but for our audience or, in her case, passengers.

If you're working from home and are regularly online and presenting virtually, then invest in good lighting. As a minimum, a backlight. Note: a backlight is not the same as a ring light. The backlight is there to gently illuminate behind you. The ring light in front means people can see you properly. This is a quality ring light, which you can adjust from cool, bright white light to warm, soft yellow light, to put directly in front of you. Small ones can sit behind your laptop; the large floor-standing ring lights favoured by influencers can also hold your phone. You can find an up-to-date list of useful products at the following websites, **www.masterclass.co.uk** and **https://masterclass.co.uk/top-tips-for-presenting-virtually**.

The art of looking good

Looking good is important. Invest in yourself and it will pay dividends. I've worked with many speakers who feel they shouldn't be judged by their image; politicians who are frustrated that people fixate on their choice of suit or hairstyle; senior executives and board members who believe it's their ideas, not the colour and cut of their jacket or shade of lipstick, that matter. I agree – it can seem shallow to be judged on looks alone, but still we judge and we are judged. Make sure you look your best, and remember: it's not about you, it's for your audience. It's about them.

Jeff Bezos reportedly said, 'Your brand is what people say about you when you're not in the room.'[13] Think about the words you would like your audience to use to describe you. If you want them to think of you as competent and professional – make sure your outfit backs that image up. If you want to be known as engaging and interesting – wear some block colours to stand out. If you're working on Zoom or Teams, invest in lighting so that you look healthy and well, not tired or out of focus.

When I work with politicians in the run up to elections, we are often restricted on budget and what they can spend on clothing, but I have to get them camera ready for TV, press interviews, hustings and all the challenges of the campaign trail. To do this, we have to be super selective about what they wear (TK Maxx and charity shops are great – just be prepared for a lot of rummaging). When I was working with Sir Nick Clegg in preparation for the very first televised election debate, we found him a brilliant suit, shirt and tie combination off the peg at Marks & Spencer. If you

---

13   J Avery, R Greenwald, 'A new approach to building your personal brand' (Harvard Business Review, May-June 2023), https://hbr.org/2023/05/a-new-approach-to-building-your-personal-brand, accessed 6 March 2025

watch the video of him speaking that night, you will see how good he looked.[14]

It can be done.

Invest in a small number of good outfits that really work for you. Don't buy any item that requires you to lose weight before you can wear it. A recent TV interview with a high-profile member of the House of Lords was completely spoiled by his shirt. It was far too tight, and as the buttons strained, he flashed the flesh and it was impossible to concentrate on what he was saying. All I kept thinking was, 'Those buttons are going to ping any minute now...'

Should you be formal or dress down? My advice: if in doubt, dress up and be more formal. No one will be offended if you're a little over dressed, and it's always easy to dress down – remove the tie, take off the jacket, roll up your sleeves – if the situation demands. It's much more difficult to dress up from down.

FROM MY HANDS TO YOURS

Mindset

- Looking good, feeling good. Invest in yourself so that when you speak and present, you know that you look good, the outfit you've chosen is flattering and it will boost your confidence.

---

14   ITV, 'The First Election Debate' (2010), www.youtube.com/watch?v=rk5HvJmy_yg, accessed 31 March 2025

Toolset

- How you stand, how you breathe, how you sit (BBC and FFOF) all matter. Great posture not only helps you deliver what you say well, it also makes you look more energised and impactful.

- Consider having your colours done. Invest in a personal shopper if the budget permits, so that you are clear what colours suit you best and what shape and cut of clothing works for your body shape. When you find your best version of you, you will have presence and confidence and, even better, you'll spend less on clothes. What's not to like?

Skillset

- As with all tools, practise the ones we've covered in this chapter every day. Use BBC when you're in a regular meeting so that it becomes something you do every time you take a seat. Know where your feet are – FFOF. Be conscious about your hands, how you hold them and how you shake them out to get rid of the excess adrenaline.

- Video yourself so that you can see more objectively how you're coming across. No one else needs to watch it – only you!

7
From Mumbling To Mastery

If you don't like the sound of your own voice – you're not alone. John Lennon and Jimi Hendrix famously hated theirs,[15] and yet their fans adored them. I don't like how I sound. Apparently, many famous actors don't like their voices, either.

Not liking our own voice is known as 'voice confrontation'. Most of us, to some extent, don't like what we hear when we listen back to a presentation or even our own telephone messages. Somehow, it just doesn't sound quite as we expected; it doesn't sound like us.

---

15 D Westbo, 'Although we love them, these singers don't like their own voice' (TheThings, 21 June 2022), www.thethings.com/8-singers-who-dont-like-their-own-voice, accessed 7 March 2025

If you'd like to understand more about why this is, there are two great TED talks that I highly recommend.[16,17] These will reassure you that if you don't like what you hear when you listen to your own voice, it's OK.

I'm not here to change your voice – it's what makes you, you – but I do want to help you ensure that it is working *for* you when you present. There are tools and techniques that are easy to use, so if you are nervous (and remember, it's OK to be nervous), you'll know what to do to come across with greater presence, confidence and authority.

We'll explore ways to alter the pace at which you speak so that people can follow you easily. We'll look at what you can do in the moment to adjust your volume and your timbre, making what you have to say truly engaging. You'll see how the power of the pause can give you credibility, presence and charisma.

There are many YouTube videos and TED talks you can watch to learn how to project your voice. One of my favourites comes from Julian Treasure – his TED

16 R Kleinberger, 'Why you don't like the sound of your own voice' (TEDxBeaconStreet, November 2017), www.ted.com/talks/rebecca_kleinberger_why_you_don_t_like_the_sound_of_your_own_voice?language=en

17 W LeBorgne, 'Vocal branding beyond words: How your voice shapes your communication' (TEDxUCincinnati, February 2018), www.ted.com/talks/wendy_leborgne_vocal_branding_beyond_words_how_your_voice_shapes_your_communication_image

talk is inspiring and easy to put into practice, too.[18] Check him out and try what he suggests – it works.

Welcome to the 5Ps of sounding good

Let's focus on five aspects that I've found make a big difference to the way you come across and can be easily worked on. These are my 5Ps:

- Pace

- Prosody

- Power

- Pause

- Pitch

We'll take each one and work on simple exercises to help you give your voice that something extra.

When we're nervous, adrenaline and our amygdala will be doing their best to protect us. Our heart rate rises to make it easier for us to run away, while also making our voice breathy and harder to project. We rush our words to get to the end of our presentation so we can leave the stage and make our escape. Our

---

18 J Treasure, 'How to speak so that people want to listen', (TEDGlobal, June 2013), www.ted.com/talks/julian_treasure_how_to_speak_so_ that_people_want_to_listen

voice dries up when we're crippled with fear, making it difficult to project with volume.

You can improve much of this through controlling your breathing using the techniques I shared with you in Chapter 5. Work on your breathing first, and then find a quiet space and go through each P in your own time.

Pace

People typically speak at around 110–150 words per minute. If you're asked to deliver a ten-minute speech, logically, your script needs to be somewhere between 1,100 and 1,500 words, but that's not the whole story. You may need to allow for laughter from your audience, time for people to take in what you have said.

You'll want to vary your pace, too. You'll sound dull and your audience will get bored if the pace is the same throughout. If you're always enthusiastic and energetic, you may exhaust them. There are times when you need to speed up or generate excitement about a topic, and times when you must slow down, pause, give the audience time to listen more intently, allowing what you say to sink in.

My paternal grandmother had incredible presence and yet was always softly spoken, she never rushed her words. A brilliant mathematician, she gained a first at Edinburgh at a time when very few women even went to university. Having had seven sons, perhaps her way of speaking was a strategy she had developed. She could command the entire room with her gentle voice and expressive hands.

We don't have to shout to have presence. The secret to having presence through our pace is to practise out loud.

Even if you don't write down exactly what you're going to say, try recording what you plan to say. Ask yourself as you listen back, is the pace right for what you're saying? Even after years of presenting, I always practise out loud to make sure my timing and my voice are right, and I have the pauses where I need them.

When you play back your recording, switch off any video so you're not distracted by how you look. You just want to hear the sound. Listen and be kind to yourself, focus on the pace and adjust as necessary.

Prosody

It's a lovely word: prosody. Its origins are in the ancient Greek word *prosodia*, which originally meant a song accompanied by music.

When we are nervous, our voice can become mono in tone (the origin of 'monotonous') and we sound flat, uninteresting, bland. Every sentence sounds like the last and, for our listeners, it's dull, but because we're nervous and don't want to draw attention to ourselves, we may be reluctant to introduce the ups and downs that create interest in our speech.

Record what you will say and listen carefully – again, switch off any video. Is there enough intonation? Where could you put more emphasis? Do you have a good mix of up and down? Be careful you don't do what I call 'the Australian' – taking your voice up at the end of every sentence as though there is a question mark there. We tend to do this when we're nervous, not sure what we're saying so the intonation goes up as though we're asking a question, even though we're not. If you want to have more impact, take your voice *down* at the end of the sentence – unless, of course, you actually are asking a question.

Power

The power in our voice comes from our ability to project, which in turn comes back to our breathing. We can talk from our nose, we can talk from our throat or let the sound come from our chest. Try each one and hear the differences. The deeper from within the chest, the more power and resonance you will have and the better your voice will sound. To have volume without coming across as though you're shouting, you have to breath more deeply from your diaphragm, pushing the sound *out* to create the power.

Just as an athlete must warm up to avoid injury and perform at their best, so we need to warm up our voice. Otherwise, we can damage it very easily. Find a quiet space and try these exercises:

1. Warm up

   - Yawn and sigh. Take in air through your nose with your mouth closed, then exhale through your nose as if you are sighing.

2. Humming

   - Place your tongue behind your bottom front teeth.

   - Hum up and down with your mouth closed (this stops you straining your voice).

3. Lip brrrr

   - Hold your lips together and make a 'brrr' sound – like a child pretending to be a car or the noise you make when you're cold.

   - Take it up and down – higher and lower – as you warm up your lips.

4. LaLaLa

   - Place your tongue behind your upper front teeth.

   - Bring it down, lowering your jaw, and make a strong laaaaa sound.

- Repeat la la la la and feel your tongue working hard.

5. Clarity

   - Repeat BDG and FTK, but pronounce them buh duh guh and fuh tuh kuh.

   - Buh, duh, guh – make the sounds using your mouth, lips and tongue.

   - Go as fast as you can – BDG, BDG, BDG, BDG.

   - Do the same for FTK.

   - Now mix the two together BDG, FTK, BDG, FTK.

6. Sing out the vowels: a e i o u. Take each one and roll with the sound:

   - Aaaaaaaa

   - Eeeeeeee

   - Iiiiiiiiiiiiiiiiiiii

   - Oooooooo

   - Uuuuuuuu

Pause

When I'm coaching, I often encourage my presenter to slow down. The use of the pause can help with that. Think of a pause as the punctuation when you speak.

You reach a full stop, you pause. A comma, you pause. Without pauses, the impact of your words is lost.

If you find it difficult to slow down (and many people do, especially when the adrenaline kicks in), then this is a great exercise for you. Simply chunk your words into small groups of three or four and introduce a pause after each group. If you have a written script or are reading notes in your slides, you can put in a marker where you want to pause.

As you pause, count one, two in your head – not out loud, obviously. It will seem a long time to you, but *not to your audience*. Pausing (and counting one, two) creates the space that allows your audience to hear, connect and comprehend what you're saying and stay with you as you speak. Record yourself and if you feel brave, share the recording with others. They will confirm that you sound much clearer and more authoritative when you pause.

In *The King's Speech*, a historical drama directed by Tom Hooper,[19] we learn how King George VI, who had a speech impediment, was helped by his voice coach to overcome his stammer by chunking the words, saying only a few at a time. It stopped the stutter, but it also helped his audiences to follow what he said, especially important with the limitations of sound

---

19   D Seidler (writer), T Hooper (director), *The King's Speech* (Momentum Pictures, Paramount, 2010)

quality in the 1930s. The pauses he introduced gave him gravitas and presence.

Look at the paragraph below – it shows how pauses can be used to give maximum impact. The aim is to make every word count, and in the following dialogue asking for a resource (the 'call to action'), this is clearly shown. As you read this aloud, count 1, 2 where you see a /, record it and listen to the impact it has on your delivery.

'This robust project plan will manage risks, / ensuring we deliver on time / and on budget. / 'Our plan is built on clear milestones, / detailed timelines, / and measurable deliverables. / Every phase of the project is carefully monitored / and adjusted as needed. 'We have included a risk strategy / which means we can address potential challenges / before they impact progress.
'Rest assured / this project will be managed with precision and discipline. / Your approval today will allow us to deliver / and give you confidence in a successful outcome.'

Pitch

When we're nervous, our voices misbehave, stripping us of presence and gravitas. You may find your voice pitching higher, becoming more squeaky. Sometimes the opposite happens and you end up sounding gruff, stilted.

As before, we must warm up our voices, breathe from our diaphragm – not the upper respiratory tract – and work on our pitch. Not everyone has that beautiful hot chocolate tone, but we can all improve our pitch.

This technique *must* be done out loud. Don't try doing it in your head. Find a quiet place where you can practise and record yourself so that you can hear the difference. Only you need to listen – you can delete it afterwards!

Breathe in through your nose, taking a deep breath from your diaphragm. Start in your normal speaking voice and count down from ten, saying each number out loud:

- **Ten**: Normal speaking voice.

- **Nine**: Take the pitch down a little bit.

- **Eight**: Take it down a bit more.

- **Seven**: Down a bit more, but be careful here. Don't go too deep too quickly, and if at any point you feel your voice straining, move back up one number.

- **Six**: If you feel comfortable and there's no strain, come down to here.

I have never had anyone go below six without straining.

In my workshops, most people find their best speaking pitch to be seven or eight – a little deeper than their conversational voice, giving more resonance. Don't overdo it; your voice must remain natural, never strained. Remember, you can easily damage your voice.

Practise this and you will find that you can bring in a more resonant pitch just by taking your voice down a couple of counts. It's also another good way to manage nerves. Watch early videos of Margaret Thatcher, and then compare them with how she sounded later in life. Her pitch got lower over the years, which was said to give her much greater presence.

You owe it to yourself to work on and protect your voice. It's a powerful machine and it's what makes you, you. Find the exercises that work best for you and create your own routine to warm up your voice and deliver with impact. You can do your warm up while holding your power pose.

FROM MY HANDS TO YOURS

Mindset

- It's wise to invest time in sounding good. This is not about vanity – you owe it to your audience to speak in a clear tone that they can hear, understand and relate to. Being nervous is perfectly normal, so don't beat yourself up. Accept that to perform at your best, you need a little pre-work.

Toolset

- Start with your breathing exercises. Whether you use 4 × 4 or others that work for you, the aim is to make it a habit and be able to breathe from your diaphragm wherever you are. This will give you greater projection, boost volume and make your voice more resonant, too.

- Work on the 5Ps – pace, prosody, power, pause, pitch. Each one will help you have a beautiful speaking voice. Don't change your voice or try to do away with your natural accent or style. Remember, your voice is what makes you, you. Just make it the best version of you.

- There are great speech therapists and voice coaches, so if you're concerned, find one. Actors do it all the time, nothing to be ashamed of.

Skillset

- We speak every day, but we don't necessarily present every day. Use your daily activities – a team meeting, a phone call, a Zoom session – to work on the 5Ps so that when you come to present, you can quickly get ready and sound great.

8
Memorable – For
The Right Reasons

We want our presentation to be memorable, for the right reasons. We don't want to be the one whose slides wouldn't work, who ran out of time or tried to tell a joke that wasn't funny, or – heaven forbid – the speaker who fell off the stage at a sales conference while still whammed from an all-nighter in the hotel bar. Yes, I was there and to this day, I can't for the life of me remember what he was speaking about, but I do remember his spectacular fall from grace.

Our job when we present is to create a little bit of magic – to be interesting, engaging, easy to follow and memorable, even if we are simply hosting a team meeting or asking for budget approval. To create that magic, have presence and be memorable – for the right reasons – it helps to know how our memory works.

How we remember things

Close your eyes and think back to your earliest memory as a child. Mine is being in a snowdrift outside our family home and being dug out by my father who was wearing a scratchy tweed jacket. I was three years old. I can still feel myself in that situation and the jacket against my face as he picked me up.

Our long-term memories are nearly always those based on experience, what happened. There's a reason for that.

There are two types of long-term memory: explicit and implicit. Explicit long-term memories are ones we consciously take time to form and recall. We repeat and use certain phone numbers, so they become part of our explicit memory. Our memory will store significant milestones – our first day at school, how it felt to pass our driving test or graduate (the experience more than the actual date), our wedding day – and things that we had to learn by rote at school – the periodic table, sections of Shakespeare, times tables.

Implicit memory is less consciously stored – it's simply there and we can, sometimes surprisingly, tap into it many years later. Know how to darn a sock, Izzy? Good grief, yes, I was taught as a child, but haven't had to do it in years… In fact, I can darn ballet pointe shoes, too.

Maybe you learned to ride a bicycle as a child, but didn't do it again until your twenties. You might have wobbled a bit the first time you got back on, but you could do it. The how-to is saved in your *implicit* long-term memory.

Think how many PowerPoint presentations you've sat through over the years. How many stand out? How many can you recall? Probably very few, if any. They will have blurred into the mists of time, all detail lost.

Short-term memory is where information goes first. It is our limited capacity to remember a small number of items for a very short period – it's at work now as you read this chapter. Our short-term memory functions long enough to remember who wants what when we order a round of drinks, or key in an authentication number or code for a payment authorisation, but try and recall that number even a few minutes later, or which variety of coffee Sharon takes (flat white, extra shot, extra hot – but then we've had a lot of coffees together so for me, it's an explicit long-term memory) and it's gone. Short-term memory is just that, short term, unless we do something with it.

For us to retain information, we need to transfer it from our short-term to our medium-term, and from there to our long-term memory. To do that initial transfer, we might repeat the information several times – usually at least three times is needed. We might choose to do that out loud or write the information down to help reinforce it. When I was in primary school, I would write out my spelling test words every Thursday night, several times if necessary, and I never got one wrong at the Friday morning test. One of the few things at school I was any good at.

You might ask people to test you on your memory to help with recall, but you must be motivated to want to do so (I really wanted that star for 10/10 on my spelling test). Let's be realistic, though – how motivated is your audience going to be to make that effort on your behalf?

As a speaker, you can't force your audience to do these things – repeat after me, write this down, let me test you. You must help them remember through your delivery and flow. That's why we have the D in our ABCD introduction – we set up our audience for what's coming by signposting the direction. We then share our limited number of key points – no more than two or three, or they won't be able to remember them – in the body of our talk, then summarise, which gives us a third chance to share the information. Finally, we restate our call to action (direction) so that people know what's expected of them.

If you follow this process as a speaker, you give your audience at least three chances to remember what you said while helping them to move your information from short to medium and then, potentially, to their long-term memory.

Some speakers use this chunking three-part approach:

- Tell the audience what you are going to tell them.

- Tell them.

- Then tell them what you just told them.

We want more than to have our message sitting around in the short term or medium-term memory. We want our message to get into our audience's long-term memory, and for the right reasons.

Circuits of neurons in the brain, known as neural networks, are created, altered or strengthened when we receive information or need to remember something. The neurons in these circuits communicate with one another through junctions called synapses. New proteins are created, and we experience an electrochemical transfer across these junctions when we repeat the information.

The more we can help our audience *experience* something (remember your earliest memories?), the longer it sticks. If we experience making a cake rather than just reading a recipe book or watching someone else make it, we are better able to recall the recipe and method, even if we can't remember every ingredient. If we experience something directly by having a go or indirectly by relating to an experience that someone else had ('I can relate to that'), it speeds up the set-up of our neural networks. We can't learn to ride a bicycle or become a great presenter by reading a manual or this book alone – we must experience doing it, have a go, experiment with ideas, get feedback, try again.

The irony is we learn more from our mistakes than we do when things go well. Watch a small child learning to walk – they fall, get up and try again, avoiding making the same mistake. I soon learned how to brake and stay upright on my motorbike as a teenager after losing control and falling into some rose bushes.

Make your message stick in the audience's memory

There's a great book that I recommend by Dan and Chip Heath called *Made to Stick*.[20] In it, the authors share six ways to make your message 'sticky' and memorable. Their checklist neatly creates the acronym SUCCES:

Simplicity

When presenting, we need to make sure that our message, and how it is delivered, is simple. That's why I encourage you to stick to two or, at most, three key points. If you confuse your audience by giving them too much (even with the best intentions), you risk them suffering from cognitive overload and forgetting it all.

---

20 D Heath, C Heath, *Made to Stick: Why some ideas take hold and others come unstuck* (Arrow, 2008)

Unexpected

If every presentation follows the same format, they blur into one. This can easily happen if you are involved in regular meetings – I see this often at board meetings. A format is agreed, a corporate template issued with spreadsheets in the same colour, font and style, and is then rolled out, again and again, at every meeting. Same slides, colours, agenda, handouts, timing – even the same seating plan, room layout and refreshments.

If you want to stand out and be memorable, then introduce something new and different into your presentation. You can do that and still respect the format. I remember a brilliant presentation about a new operating system delivered by a geeky engineer using two hand puppets talking to one another. Totally unexpected, original and always remembered. We – the audience – experienced something new.

Concrete

How do we make what we talk about concrete?

Our brains are wired to remember hard examples – we zone out when a speaker talks about concepts or slips into jargon. According to a recent study by Preply, the most common business jargon phrases in use currently are 'for your information (FYI)', 'at the end of the day', 'think outside the box', 'touch base' and 'circle back'.[21] No wonder we zone out – what are they talking about? Rather than waffle, give concrete examples that your audience can relate to.

When I was running a leadership programme at the probation service, one of the desired outcomes was to reduce the high levels of stress-related sickness absence. As leaders applied the techniques I shared, they saw significant reductions and great results.

Presenting back, I showed that these absence rates had gone down from over 4,200 days per year to under 2,500. Yes, a big number, but it was hard to relate to. Then the HR director found a way.

'This means,' he said, 'we now have an additional eight probation officers at work *every day*, dealing with offenders.' Brilliant, concrete, clear. Everyone in the room could picture what that looked like. That's what stuck.

When two toy-manufacturing companies merged, their executives were brought together to find a way to combine their strengths. The companies were totally different in both the types of toys they produced and their culture.

---

21 Preply, 'Study Reveals the Most Annoying Corporate Jargon' (no date), https://preply.com/en/learn/best-and-worst-corporate-jargon, accessed 31 March 2025

As the executive teams gathered for their first merger meeting, a surprise awaited them. On each chair was a wrapped parcel, but they were instructed not to open them yet. The speaker began by framing the challenge ahead: how do we merge two distinctly different companies into a cohesive unit?

With anticipation building and everyone intrigued to know what was in the parcels, he finally invited the audience to unwrap them. To their surprise, half the group had boldly painted action figures made by one company, half unwrapped soft primary-coloured educational toys from the other. This contrast served as a powerful representation of the companies' differences, prompting discussions on how to bridge the gap between their unique identities and find common ground.

Not only was it memorable (no one had ever done anything like that before), this presentation provided a powerful visual of what the differences were.

Credible

You now know it's important that you blow your own trumpet (even just a little bit) as a speaker, and that I encourage you to include the C – your credentials – in your ABCD introduction. Your audience needs to know that you're qualified to speak on your topic.

You can talk about yourself, but credibility can come from a third party, too. Examples at an interview of where you've done similar work before boost your credibility; a client story where you've made a difference will help your sales pitch. Having a proxy in your audience to confirm that what you're proposing has worked is another way. People don't just believe you; they believe what others say *about* you. That's why we read reviews, use TripAdvisor or search out Michelin-starred restaurants.

Emotional

Think of all the ways we are influenced or persuaded through our emotions. The cute puppy dog that unrolls the toilet paper in the TV advert – not that funny if it actually happens to you… A charity request that pulls at our heart strings, making it impossible to walk by without donating.

We are influenced by emotions, less so by logic and numbers. Connecting to people's feelings will make what you say more memorable and create a sense of intimacy. One of the best ways to do this is through stories.

Stories

Facts tell, but stories sell. A story that supports your message drives action from your audience because they can see for themselves how what you're suggesting can work. When people relate to a story, either because it's like something they've faced, or because it connects to a problem or need that they, too, have, you get what I call the 'virtual nod'. Everyone tunes in to stories – they're what we're brought up on as children.

Many of the people I work with are involved in business presentations – sales pitches, funding requests, applying for a job or a promotion. Others, particularly politicians I coach, are looking to influence voters or secure the nomination for a constituency. In both cases, a good story helps people to see what's possible.

If you're at a wedding or funeral, you'll know how stories make a speech or eulogy powerful, entertaining and memorable – reducing people to tears and laughter. A good story touches our emotions, builds credibility, is concrete, often unexpected in today's business world, and is simple and easy to understand – ticking all the boxes in SUCCES by Dan and Chip.

Stories and the Trust Equation

Stories help what you say stick and be more memorable. Like following a recipe, you need to try telling stories, practise them, find what works for you, your personality and style. Preparing your stories can't be left to chance or the last minute; you must invest the time beforehand.

Sharing stories and experiences (some organisations may call them 'use cases', 'citations' or 'case studies' – don't worry about the terminology) is one of the quickest and easiest ways to build trust, create rapport and empathy, and demonstrate that you have your audience's best interests at heart. Let's go back to the Trust Equation from Chapter 2. If we break down the components, you can see how a story can support all four elements.

1. **Credibility:** A story shows that you know what you're talking about; you've worked in a similar sector/industry/market; you understand the world your audience inhabits and the challenges faced; you realise that every situation is unique.

2. **Reliability:** A story demonstrates that you've done similar things before; you've proven you can do it. What you're saying to your audience is, 'You're safe with me'. You've delivered; you did what you said you would do and can be relied on.

3. **Intimacy:** By recounting how you have supported individuals in similar situations, you convey to your audience a sense of empathy and understanding. This not only illustrates that you have their back, but also helps the audience see that they are not alone in their struggles. It emphasises your genuine intention to help, creating a safe space where they can be seen, heard and valued.

4. **Self-orientation:** When we share a real story (warts and all) with honesty and integrity, our self-orientation is perceived as low – we're

sharing this story to help others. This isn't merely about recounting our experiences; it's about a narrative that serves a greater purpose: to uplift, inspire and support the audience. We create a connection that says, 'This isn't about me; it's about you and your journey.' The story shows that we get what their concerns, issues and needs are.

As always, it's not about us, it's about our audience

As children, we learn through stories. We are entertained and we feel safe and comfortable with the formula: 'Once upon a time... in a far-off land... Good overcomes evil, and they all lived happily ever after.'

The power of the 5D framework

Every compelling story has five components. To make this easier to remember, I've created a framework used by thousands of people where each component starts with a D – description, dilemma, desire, delivered, differentiator. It will help you build your library of stories quickly and easily.

However, there's another very important D. The sixth D stands for *discipline* – discipline to prepare your stories in advance and to practise them so that they become a natural part of your presentation or talk. You can't *tell* a story if you don't *know* the story. That's why discipline matters.

Fun fact – I was told by a now retired police inspector that one of the best ways to see if someone is lying is to get them to tell their story in reverse. If it's full of inconsistencies and lies, it will be very difficult to tell backwards. If the story is true, the chances are they'll be able to do it.

The moral here? Know your story, especially under a police caution…

My 5D method gives your stories a structure and logical flow. With a portfolio of stories, you can then draw on them for different presentation scenarios. You will see how you can headline from any one of the 5Ds, which will allow you to use the same story in more than one situation while making it directly relevant to your audience.

A great story allows you to show off, but in a nice and professional way – what I call 'evidence-based bragging'. A good 5D story helps your audience to relate to you and to make what you say memorable. You're more likely to get the virtual nod because they see in your story problems or issues similar to those that they face, too. That creates a special intimacy – a key element in building trust. They experience through your storytelling what other people went through, creating a connection and a deeper shared understanding.

Dilemma ❷
The problem was...
The issue they faced... .

Desire ❸
What they wanted...
What they needed was..

❶ **Description**
The context,
customer/client
situation

❹ **Delivered**
What we did for them
was...

Differentiator ❺
Why XXX?
The value and contribution
we delivered
(tangible, measurable, #, $, €, %)

Draw a big 5 on a notepad or a large Post-it note –
I recommend at least A5 size. Start top right, follow
the numbers and work through each of the 5Ds.

Description

The first D sets the context and describes what's to
come. If sharing a business story, we might use the
organisation's name. If it's a well-known and successful organisation, that boosts credibility.

If I'm talking to a law firm, the audience will be comfortable if they know that Masterclass has worked
with other law firms. When I'm talking to my pros-
pects about personal impact and presentation skills
coaching, they're reassured to know I've worked

with high-profile business leaders in their industry or trained well-known politicians or TV pundits.

The first D answers the question: 'Where have you done something like this (the audience's need – remember those bleeps on the radar) before?' The description is about context, so keep it brief. If the organisation or person in your story is a household name, you don't need to explain who they are. 'We recently did a project with Ikea – have you heard of them? They're a...' No! However, if you have recently worked with a particular division of Ikea, you would add that information.

If you're using a customer for your story that is not well-known, then it's appropriate to share more information: what they do, the size of the business, turnover, where they sit in the sector, who their customers are. The key is to make sure that you show a connection with the person or audience you're talking to so that they can see the relevance.

If I'm presenting to a company involved in research, analytics or retail, or whose clients are in the fast-moving consumer goods (FMCGs) (think shampoo, food) industry, then this example would be relevant and credible:

'We recently worked with ABC, a data-analytics company headquartered in New York with operations around the world. They specialise in gathering sales data from supermarkets and pharmacies, and their clients include companies such as L'Oréal, Gillette...'

People listening now get what the company does, even if they haven't previously heard the name or had any direct dealings with them.

Remember to keep your first D relatively brief, it's to provide context and help position what you want to share. It's not a complete description or detailed explanation, but it's important because it's helping build your credibility, reliability and that sense of intimacy from the Trust Equation we talked about previously.

Dilemma

In the second D of our story, we share the issues, challenges or problems that an organisation or individual had. Maybe a technical issue, revenue was down or they had to improve productivity. The dilemma is a great way to connect intimately with the audience you're talking to. If they face a similar issue or problem to what you're describing, you show you understand and relate to what they're going through.

It's not appropriate to launch into confidential detail on the problems the other party faced. To do so risks you coming across as indiscreet and unprofessional, spoiling that sense of intimacy. Overshare confidential information and you'll rapidly break trust.

Taking our example further:

> 'ABC was facing several challenges. They were losing market share to a competitor that was aggressively undercutting their prices. If they lost a client, it would mean they couldn't bid on that contract again for at least two years.
>
> 'Furthermore, their technical analysts found themselves having to negotiate with professional buyers rather than directly with marketing teams who appreciated the value of their data. This shift was particularly intimidating for the analysts because they were neither comfortable nor trained to work with such strong, often hard-nosed buyers.'

If you've chosen the right story, the audience you're sharing it with will be starting to nod. If not physically, then definitely virtually!

Desire

When we talk about desire, we show empathy and awareness of what our audience might be experiencing, allowing us to connect even more deeply. Just as in a fairy tale, we share how good (the desire) overcomes evil (the dilemma).

Let's take our ABC example:

'What ABC wanted (desire) was to secure revenue by retaining key client contracts when they came up for renewal. They called this "contract retention". If a big client terminated their contract, they couldn't recover from that quickly and, worse, would have to wait at least two years before they could try to win it back.

'ABC wanted their people to get away from negotiating on price, and instead show the value that their services delivered. Every time they got into a price discussion, their much bigger competitor would undercut them. Additionally, they wanted to help their people negotiate confidently with professional buyers – something they'd never done before.'

In commercial organisations, the desire phase will often be around wanting to grow revenue, increase profits, improve earnings before interest, taxes, depreciation and amortisation (EBITDA), cash flow, bid to win ratios, contract retention, employee turnover, productivity or performance – what we might call tangible measures or results. The things you considered on the left-hand side of your audience's radar when you were planning.

It can also be about feelings – those intangible measures, the personal wins that we recorded on the right-hand side of the radar. It's easier to talk about the emotions of someone else rather than assuming you know the emotions of the person/people in front of you.

I might use my third-party example with an audience:

> 'ABC's HR director was concerned how they
> could retain analysts in the business. It was
> an anxious time for him. One of his personal
> objectives was to reduce staff turnover and
> attrition from 32% to less than 18% that fiscal
> year and he needed to find a way to do this.'

I'm not saying, 'I bet you're worried about staff turn-over and losing some of your best people. Must be very stressful right now for you. Is your job at risk if you fail to sort this out? Is your bonus out of the window?' By sharing what happened to someone else in a similar situation, I help my audience to experience through my story how it might be for them if they work with me.

Delivered

In this part of our story, the fourth D, we talk about what we *did* or what we *delivered*. Remember this is about sharing an interesting and compelling story to influence your audience and help them retain your key points. It is not a full report on every detail about who did what, when.

It can be tempting during the delivered part to go into detail, often with good intentions and a desire to share as much as possible. That's because this is probably the part of the story that you're most interested in yourself. After all, it's what you did.

Remember cognitive overload? Your audience doesn't need all that detail. The more you give, the less they remember. If you're droning on about every aspect, they're probably too polite to tell you to stop, but they'll stop listening. If you go on at length, what's your level of self-orientation? For whose benefit is the detail? Are you simply indulging yourself because this is what you find most interesting?

Keep the fourth D, delivered, at a high level, but with enough detail to connect to your audience's situation. Make it personal and relevant so that they can see how a similar approach could work for *them*. Stick to the facts, a brief journey or roadmap, and keep it short.

With my ABC story, I could say:

> 'To grow revenue and improve contract retention – the two things that mattered most to the CEO – we designed a training programme working with their country managers across Europe. Over six months, we ran a series of workshops in each country where the managers learned how to build deeper relationships and show the value ABC's services delivered, not just the cost. Each country manager was trained to support

their teams and took part in the sessions committed to coaching the techniques and using the materials afterwards – all of which were produced in local languages.'

The purpose of our story is to connect with our audience on issues that matter to them and to help achieve the outcomes we want. I could say much more about what we did, but unless the audience specifically asks, I keep it brief.

Differentiator

The differentiator is so much more than 'and they all lived happily ever after...' It's the point that truly differentiates your story, makes you stand out and will stick in the memory of your audience.

To have a clear differentiator, you must think ahead. In the ABC example, I knew that revenue and contract retention were the most important metrics for the CEO. They were big bleeps on his radar. We established that during our exploratory phase. At that time, he didn't say he needed a training programme as such, but he knew he had a problem and that he had to grow revenue, retain contracts and help his consultants negotiate with professional buyers.

The more we showed results of the programme, the more valuable it was to the CEO. It addressed the results and personal wins on his radar.

The differentiator part of the story, the fifth D, is where you can brag or boast a little. If you don't blow your own trumpet, who will? The CEO of ABC could demonstrate to his board in the USA that he'd delivered great results – growth in revenue, improvements in contract retention, keeping good people. For my company, we were able to speak about the impact our training had when talking to other clients.

I have a wonderful dentist called David. Originally from New York, he's worked in Denmark and is recognised internationally by his peers as a top practitioner in his field. When I was a student, I played a lot of lacrosse – a vicious but marvellous game where you can get knocked around a bit. That, combined with some poor dental treatment, meant my teeth needed a little work. I consulted David about what he could do. As it turned out, quite a lot.

He wasn't cheap, but it was worth it. Now every time I go for my check-up, the first thing he says as he peers into my mouth is, 'Gee, I did a good job with those teeth!' He reminds me, very beautifully, what a good decision I made going to him in the first place and how even he can hardly see the white fillings replacing the grey ones. He's blowing his own trumpet, I love him for it and I recommend him to everyone.

The best and most memorable differentiators will be the impressive tangible gains and results that you deliver. With ABC, I can say, 'Within twelve months of starting the Masterclass programme, ABC had grown revenues by $55 million and was at 97% contract retention levels – the highest ever in the company's history.' It may not always be possible to have a big number, but the more you show the value, the return on investment and how what you did made a difference, the more powerful and memorable your story will be.

I was working with a team who dealt with mergers and acquisitions, helping clients buy and sell companies. They had loads of stories, but they were hardly using them. When they did, much of the focus was on the fourth D, what they delivered. This was the part that *they* were most interested in.

When I probed deeper, I found they had some fantastic differentiators. There were deals where the client had achieved increased revenues in the millions. Due diligence work that meant a buyer had saved millions when buying an asset. Deals that opened new markets, increased share prices and resulted in multi-million projects.

There are situations where we perhaps don't know about the differentiator. We complete our work, we move on, and yet... by going back and talking with that client, we find out they've gone on to achieve great things. Maybe they've reduced staff attrition levels, saving thousands, or, as in the case of ABC, retained clients and improved customer satisfaction and net promoter scores.

You can also share some intangible gains as differentiators. The consultants at ABC were much more confident and therefore enjoyed their work more following our training. They were no longer intimidated by procurement. Another client said the best bit about a recent project was that he got his weekends back. For him, that was the greatest differentiator of all.

Build your library of stories

Remember the sixth D, discipline? No one can build your stories for you. To be a good speaker, you need a library of great stories that you can use in different situations.

If you are delivering business presentations or sales pitches, your best stories will be projects you successfully completed with other clients and the challenges you helped them overcome. If you are going for a promotion or job interview, your stories should include examples of where you delivered results in a previous role and demonstrated the skills, competencies and behaviours that this new role requires. How you dealt with difficult people; your creativity; how you maintained resilience during tough times; how you inspired others as a leader.

As a politician, you need stories that illustrate the struggles that your constituents and voters experience, and how your work and policies have helped and will help in the future. When you're looking to inspire your team as a leader, your stories are a brilliant way to illustrate their great work, the pride you have in them or where someone's behaviour played out an important value that your organisation stands for.

If you're delivering a wedding speech or a eulogy, your stories will endear you to your listeners. Make sure they show the character, personality and traits of the happy couple or the deceased. If you want to take to the stage as a comedian – you're going to need loads of stories.

For a great example of comic storytelling, look up recordings of Janey Godley, a hugely talented Scottish comedian who was taken too soon by cancer. Alternatively, go back to your own favourite performers and listen again. You'll probably find it's the stories that not only amuse you, but endear you to them, too.

Rehearse your stories

'It's the way I tell 'em,' Frank Carson, comedian, was famous for saying.

A great story takes time to build, needs structure and a logical flow (5D does that for you), but the magic comes through your *telling* of it. To do that well, you need rehearsal and practice. Frank Carson was right – it *is* the way you tell 'em.

We've talked about how great speakers make story-telling look natural, and we can easily fall for thinking that this just happens for them. It doesn't; they too must rehearse and practise.

I find it's much easier to visualise your story if you capture it using the big figure 5.

You can check you have all the components; you can see the flow from 'once upon a time' (first D, description) to 'and they all lived happily ever after' (the fifth D, differentiator); and you can now headline from any one of the 5Ds. This is so powerful because it means that one 5D story can be used in many different situations.

Headlining from any of the 5Ds

The natural flow of a story starts with a description, continues with the desire and dilemma, explains what you did or delivered, and ends with a strong differentiator. Depending on your presentation and your desired outcomes, you can headline from any one of the 5Ds, so having the story laid out using your large 5 makes it easier to visualise them all.

You may be presenting to an audience in a particular industry or sector – financial services, distribution, law. This means that when you headline from any part of your story of working with a similar organisation (bank, retailer, law firm), you have a highly relevant starting point.

Description

'Let me share something we did recently for another law firm…' Think back to your Trust Equation. When you show that you've done something for a similar organisation or individual, you demonstrate credibility, that you can be relied on and that your audience will be safe with you.

Dilemma

People like to know that you 'get' what you're talking about, that you've had similar experiences or challenges to the ones they're facing right now. For example, 'You mentioned the issue about not having the skills in house for this project. We recently worked with a client who faced a similar challenge…' Here you link what someone else was concerned with in a similar situation to your audience's needs, helping them to feel supported and know that you clearly understand and empathise with what they're going through.

Desire

'I know it's important for you and the board that this product is released on time, given the market pressures. Let me show you how we've done this with another client so you can be confident in what we're proposing...' Again, you're demonstrating that you understand – indeed, empathise with – what your audience is facing, and you have experience of succeeding in a similar matter before.

Delivered

People you present to want to be confident that you know what you're doing. We often talk about warts and all. They want to know that you've walked in their shoes, experienced similar struggles, that you have skin in the game.

'Managing a project as complex as this, staying on budget and delivering on time, is tricky. This is something I had to deal with recently in my current role where we had tight deadlines and had to stay on track. Let me share with you how I went about that...' You are reassuring your audience (in this case, interviewer(s)) that you understand their issues and have a way of dealing with them that works.

Differentiator

Finally, you can headline from the fifth D, starting with your differentiator and what you did that made a difference. It can often be the most powerful headline of all.

'Does coaching really work? It does – we helped a major client secure a $1billion ten-year contract as a result of coaching their team for the final board pitch. Let me share with you how we did it…'

Three-part messaging to make a point really stick

Stories help to make your message stick, and a good story explains why what you're suggesting can work. In journalistic training, there is a great technique: three-part messaging. I call it point, story, point.

Remember the power of three? By repeating something, typically three times, we are more likely to remember it. The three-part messaging technique does that by introducing a metaphor or simile to help move what we say to our audience's long-term memory. A simile is a figure of speech that compares one thing to another, typically using 'as' or 'like', while a metaphor states that two apparently different things are the same, that one is representative of the other. For example:

- It's really tough right now. It's like trying to build the pyramids. (S)

- She's as quiet as a mouse. (S)

- Shakespeare's 'All the world's a stage'. (M)

- Time is money. (M)

When we use similes and metaphors, we are helping our audience to see, hear and experience what we're saying by building their own picture or understanding of what we're talking about.

We can also use stories and anecdotes to make a point stick. Let's say I want a leadership team to know about my colleagues and that they deserve to be recognised at a sales conference. I could just say they've been great, please nominate them for the Sales Team of the Year. Meh. If I want my message to stick, I use three-part messaging (point, story, point). Note the use of the phrase *so that* as I link my story to my concluding point.

- **Point:** 'This team has been fantastic this year, both in their results and in their attitude. They're one of the best sales teams I've ever had the honour to lead, and they deserve to be recognised at the sales conference.'

- **Story:** 'Last quarter they delivered on all their customer satisfaction metrics, exceeded their net promoter scores and closed the quarter at 120% over target on margin. They've met and gone beyond every target this financial year, and maintained their positive attitude throughout, despite it being a tough, competitive market out there.'

- **Point:** *'So that's* why I am proposing them for the Team of the Year, not just because of their results, but because of the way they delivered them.'

FROM MY HANDS TO YOURS

Mindset

- Recognise that stories, metaphors and similes have a special part in creating the magic when you present. Your ability to engage comes from sharing stories and bringing to life your experiences. It's not something you can just do – it takes time and discipline to create, rehearse and share your stories. It's what will make you stand out. Get your mindset into the discipline of preparing your stories and invest time in practising them, out loud.

Toolset

- Use the 5D framework and capture your stories with a big 5 as explained above. Remember the importance of discipline – the sixth D – in writing down and capturing your stories. No one can or will do it for you; you must create the magic with your own stories.

- Make impact using point, story, point. Be clear what the key point is you want to make and weave it into your presentations and talks by using three-part messaging. State your point, build a story, metaphor or simile that helps illustrate it, and then explain why your point makes sense, using 'so that' to land the point again. You might like to think of point, story, point as a sandwich. The point is the bread and the story the filling.

Skillset

- Remember – a skill is a technique you can use under pressure. Only *you* can build and know your stories. They are what make you unique. Get comfortable with creating your 5D and point, story, point examples. Write them down, edit them, video yourself speaking them out loud, practise again and remember the sixth D, discipline, to make sure that you always have a story you can use.

PART THREE

THE FINISHING TOUCHES THAT MAKE YOU STAND OUT

I hope that by now, you appreciate that a presentation isn't a slide deck and that the best speakers, the ones who we remember (for the right reasons) because they inspire, motivate and connect with us, don't rely on slides alone. Indeed, some of the most influential speakers, who present with great impact and presence, may not use any.

I'm not saying never use slides; I am saying reframe how you view them. They're visual aids to help your audience see and understand what you're sharing, making it better for them. They're not prompts for you.

There are times when we need to help our audience take on board what we're saying and retain our message, and that's when we bring in our slides, props, visual aids or, if we're training, models (as I've done in this book), quizzes, question and answer sessions, and discussions. Numbers, statistics, data are all clearer and easier to understand with a slide. Using a word cloud or a pie chart means we can show what the numbers and data represent, but remember these resources are all to help our audience, for their benefit, not ours.

When we present, it shouldn't be one way. To engage and connect authentically with our audience, we need to be comfortable having discussions, taking questions and encouraging debate.

In this part I will share tools to help you do just that.

9
Bringing Your Message To Life

We should make all our presentations engaging, interesting and memorable. It may be a ten-minute project update, but use the opportunity to stand out and give your audience a great, not just good, experience.

Just because we can use slides, videos and fancy graphics, it doesn't mean we always should. For many, the meaning of the word 'presentation' has become 'slide deck'. Never forget that a slide is simply a visual aid for your *audience*.

Let me repeat that. A slide is a visual aid.

You are the best visual aid of all.

I ran a Powerful Presence Masterclass recently for a group of seasoned corporate executives working for a global multi-billion-dollar business. They've seen thousands of presentations and delivered hundreds of their own.

I used very few slides over the two days. Instead, I focused on activities with whiteboards and flip charts, pictures, images and videos to bring to life what they were learning. The feedback was incredible. One of the best things? That it was such a relief to have so few slides, and yet it was easy, through the flips and images, to remember all the tools and techniques.

There's a time and a place for slides and they can be incredibly useful, but remember what a slide is: a visual aid not for you, the speaker, but for your audience. Slides are there to help your audience remember and retain your key points. To move what you say from their short-term memory to their medium and then long-term one. They're not there as a reading lesson from you, nor to show how clever and whizzy you can make them, nor as a prompt or script to remind you what to say.

Remember how we structured our diamond in Chapter 4, transferring the two or three key points to the body? We hadn't at that point even considered what slides to use, but with the bones of our presentation in place, we can now decide what visual aids or props to introduce for the *benefit of our audience*.

We looked at the power of stories in Chapter 8. In this chapter, we'll explore what else you can do to make you and what you say memorable, for the right reasons.

Golden rules for PowerPoint

If you are going to use slides, remember that less is more, and if you can, use a picture or a diagram rather than text. Microsoft have their golden rules, you can find them easily online.[22] I've summarised them here and added my own:

Golden rule #1 – Use templates

Templates – there are hundreds to choose from, but go with ones with more white space on them. The more complicated or fancy, the more you confuse your audience.

What do you want them to look at? You? The numbers? The pictures? The comments? The beauty of a template is that you have consistency in typefaces, sizes, layouts. You might not notice a slide jump from Arial to Calibri, but I can guarantee someone in the audience will, and they'll be annoyed.

---

22   D Ashby, '5 golden rules of PowerPoint design', (Microsoft 365, 30 April 2024), https://create.microsoft.com/en-us/learn/articles/5-golden-rules-powerpoint-design, accessed 10 March 2025

Golden Rule #2 - No walls of text

I was designing a workshop for a client and needed to know about their new competencies and behaviours. These, apparently, were summarised on one slide (one?) that they'd been sharing internally with stakeholders.

Oh my, there was a *lot* of text. It wasn't a slide designed for a presentation; it was a summary of information in one place. Useful if circulated internally for people to read at their leisure, but not something to use in front of an audience.

Don't be guilty of what I call 'a reading lesson with Mrs Rimmer'. Having shared it with me, the client then proceeded to read out *every single line*. I'd already finished reading the lot before they were even half-way through the first box… we've all been there.

Consider Microsoft's 5-5-5 rule. No more than five lines, no more than five words, no more than five minutes. I'd be tougher: 3-3-3 is even better. No more than three lines, no more than three words, and no more than three minutes.

If you do use text, duble cheeck speling! Spellchecker doesn't play nicely with slides. You must proof your slide deck, and then proof again. If in doubt, ask someone else to check, too. It's easy to become blind to mistakes. We know what we mean to say, so we miss the typo. 'Proffessional'? I don't think so…

Golden rule #3 – Choose your colours and fonts carefully

My brother-in-law is an eye surgeon. He reminds me that everyone, at a certain age, will need glasses.

There's nothing worse for your audience than struggling to read a tiny font or colours that they can't distinguish. Always make sure that everyone can see what's on your slides – stand at the back of the room, or on Teams, and check them yourself. Some virtual platforms may even change the fonts – especially if you're using one of the rare ones, change bullet points to a different style, mess up your formatting. Remember you may also have people in your audience with visual impairments or who are colour blind.

To be safe, go with text no smaller than 24 pts.

That's this big. Minimum.

When it comes to colour, have a clear, easy-to-read contrast. Dark backgrounds should have light font and vice versa. Again, check – if your audience can't read it, they'll zone out. Remember, the slide is for your audience's benefit, it's not a prompt for you.

Golden rule #4 – Go easy on the animation

Just because you can do fancy stuff with slides doesn't mean you should. Some animation can be effective, but don't overdo it. You want your audience to focus on you and your key points. You don't want them confused or irritated by text flying, spinning or bouncing in left, right and centre.

Ask yourself – does this animation enhance my presentation, or does it distract the audience? If in doubt, leave it out.

Here's a top tip for presenting with slides, which could be useful if you realise halfway through a presentation that you have overdone the animation or your audience is losing interest. Make sure you have my #1 PowerPoint tool up your sleeve. If you want your audience to focus on *you* and not the slide, or perhaps you jump ahead and you need to hide a slide, use the blackout feature. Press B on your keyboard or the off on your clicker if you're using one. It will make your slide screen go black. Press B again or any other key to bring it back to the slide.

If you're in an unlit room where using B would plunge everyone into darkness, use the white option. Press W and your screen will go white. Press any button to return to the slide. Rehearse so that you can use these easily.

Golden rule #5 – Do you need a slide at all?

This rule is mine, not Microsoft's: if in doubt, leave it out.

If you're presenting in person for about ten minutes, three or four slides are more than enough. If you're delivering a ninety-minute training webinar, then you will need more because there is little else for your audience to see. However, you'll be more engaging getting them to discuss and unmute using chat or breakout rooms rather than lecturing and reading from slides.

There are plenty of new apps that will help you build slides that tell a story, slides that take your audience on a journey, breathtaking and creative templates that will make you stand out. Search out ones that work for you.

Golden rule #6 – Make numbers meaningful

Think about how best to make your numbers meaningful. Our brains struggle to remember numbers. We find it easier if we can get a sense of what those numbers look or feel like. When something is as high as the Eiffel Tower (330 metres to the tip) or as long as three London buses (about 30 metres), we can picture what that means.

The best professional footballers in the UK (soccer players for my American readers) often earn an eye-watering amount of money, and so their pay scales are referred to in weekly terms. Kevin De Bruyne – one of the top players – is described as earning £400,000 a week, rather than £20.8 million a year. Still a telephone number, but easier to grasp.

Sniffer dogs are trained to find less than one teaspoon of narcotics in a million gallons of water. We know that's a lot of water, but just how much? Isn't it easier to visualise when it's described as the equivalent of two Olympic swimming pools?

A friend of mine had a Saturday job as a student at a well-known High Street retailer. One weekend, before the shop opened, the manager showed the staff a huge pile of wine and beer bottles. That pile was, he said, the value of what would typically get shop-lifted on a Saturday. The staff were shocked.

He could have just told them the value of what goes missing, but seeing what that represented – a heck of a lot of wine and beer, very relatable to the students – made it meaningful. They got it and from then on were super conscious to watch out for thefts and slippage in the store.

I mentioned colour-blind people earlier. There are over 300 million of them in the world today, nearly all men.[23] That means 8% of men globally – or to put it another way, one in twelve – will have the condition. If you're watching a men's football match, it's highly likely that at least two of the players on the pitch will be colour blind (and, as any devoted fan from the losing team will tell you, the referee will be totally blind).

---

23   Colour Blind Awareness, 'About colour blindness', www. colourblindawareness.org, accessed 10 March 2025

See what I've done there?

Make numbers meaningful for *your* audience.

Props are wonderful

The physical, tangible benefit of using a prop is powerful. It can even add interest in a virtual presentation. Sadly, it's rarely used.

One of the most powerful moments in a talk by an Olympic athlete was when he passed his gold medal around the room. We in the audience got the chance to hold it, experience it for real – and no, it didn't go missing.

With a prop, you have an opportunity to connect to your audience's senses – sight, smell, touch, hearing, maybe even taste. There are a few caveats, though:

- Your prop must be relevant to your topic. Your audience must never struggle to make the connection.

- Everyone in the audience must be able to see or hold the prop. Don't rush.

- Practise with your prop so that you are comfortable using it and it works as planned.

- Remember to put the prop away when you've made your point otherwise it becomes a distraction.

Even if you practise, things can go wrong. I watched a presenter struggle with music on his phone. The idea was good, but he couldn't get the piece he wanted to play at the right moment and it spoilt the impact. Have a back-up plan and if the prop doesn't work, move on quickly.

Go old school with a whiteboard or flip chart

We learn better from whiteboards and blackboards than other media.[24] That doesn't mean we should restrict their use to the classroom. They can be very effective online, too.

Why do they work so well?

- **Audience engagement and interaction**: A board allows for real-time content creation *with* your audience. This keeps them engaged and focused on your material.

- **Versatile, spontaneous and adaptable**: A diagram that you build with your audience can make a complex approach much easier to understand and follow.

---

24 i3-Technologies, '5 Proven Ways Interactive Whiteboards Improve Learning Outcomes' (24 May 2010), www.i3-technologies.com/en/blog/stories/education/5-proven-ways-interactive-whiteboards-improve-learning-outcomes, accessed 31 March 2025

- **Visual learning**: Whiteboards and flips fire up our ability to learn visually. We can process, retain and recall information more effectively.

- **Speak, write and read**: Drawing on a board helps our audience use multiple senses and different areas of the brain, leading to better understanding and retention.

- **Less distraction**: Unlike high-tech options with animated slides, traditional boards don't require complex setups, which means our audience stays more focused with us.

- **Simplicity**: Sometimes less is more. All you need is a working pen.

If you're worried you won't remember what goes on to your flip, draft the key points in pencil before you start. No one else will see them and you'll have the prompts you need.

Get yourself the flip pads with pre-prepared little squares printed on them. They're brilliant, allowing you to divide up your flip and keep your lines straight.

Take a class on how to write on a whiteboard. It's easy to learn and if you use a chisel tip (rather than a round tip) pen, your writing will look more professional.

Old school perhaps, but effective.

Using a range of slides, a prop, music, video, a flip chart or whiteboard means you keep your audience guessing and engaged. You're no longer guilty of 'death by PowerPoint'.

If the subject and situation allow, involve your audience. Pose questions, draw out comments, ask for questions, encourage debate. The more they engage, the more they remember you and what you have been talking about.

FROM MY HANDS TO YOURS

Mindset

- Think what you want to do to bring what you say to life. Put yourself in your audience's shoes and consider the full range of tools to engage. Don't limit yourself to slides just because everyone else does. Be different, be brave.

Toolset

- There are so many fantastic tools that you can use to make what you say memorable and you the speaker everyone remembers. Mix things up – bring in slides, use a flip chart or whiteboard, pose questions to your audience, introduce a prop and practise using it.
- Find apps and use templates that will help you create slides and animation that support your message. Don't be restricted to bullet points. Remember the golden rules.

Skillset

- Once you've decided what you want to use, practise and rehearse. Video yourself and watch it back.

- If you struggle with something or the timing doesn't work – drop it. If it didn't work in rehearsal, it's bound to fail in a live delivery.

- The same goes for using certain words. If you find you trip over a word or struggle with it when rehearsing, you can guarantee you'll trip over it again. Find another easier one.

10
Does Anyone Have A Question?

M any people worry about handling questions and what they see as the 'dreaded' question and answer (Q&A) session. I hear comments like:

- 'What if I don't know the answer?' Be prepared, but accept that you may not know. That's fine. Be honest, let the questioner know you don't have the answer yet, but will take their question on board.

- 'What if I don't get any questions?' Why? Did you bore the audience rigid? Perhaps you really did cover everything.

- 'What if they start asking questions on things that I'll talk about later?' That's why you need your ABCD introduction.

The Achilles heel is when you are asked the *one thing* that you don't want a question about, your weak spot. As with all things, success with Q&A comes from planning.

Watch a good comedian, they'll have a perfect retort to every heckler at the back. It looks effortless, but it's because they're prepared. The comedian Jo Brand says that working as a psychiatric nurse for ten years helped her build her collection of barbed put downs.[25] She'd heard all the comments (and worse) before and was ready.

When is a question really a question?

Not all questions are born equal. Our audiences ask questions for lots of reasons and not just for more information. Some questions come from a gap in understanding, but many are not questions at all. What masquerades as a question may be resistance to your idea, a different point of view or someone keen to show how much *they* know.

Listen carefully. Is it a question? If it was written down, would there be a question mark at the end of the sentence? If written in Spanish, would there be an

25 S Bains, 'Jo Brand says being spat at and fat-shaming hecklers are nothing compared to abuse she suffered in first job' (*Mirror*, 4 April 2024), www.mirror.co.uk/3am/celebrity-news/jo-brand-recalls-horror-experience-32497984, accessed 12 March 2025

upside-down question mark at the start of the sentence, too? ¿How wonderful is that?

If there's no question mark, it's not a question.

'How will you deliver the project on time?' is a question.

'I can't see how you'll deliver the project on time,' is a form of resistance or someone expressing their concern. It's not a question.

'Projects are rarely delivered on time, take it from me,' is a point of view. It's not a question.

'How much do you really know about this?' could be a boomerang question. The person asking doesn't want your experience, they want to bounce it back on themselves (hence the boomerang) so that they can talk about their experience or how much they know. Therefore, it's not really a question.

'Let's be honest, how are you ever going to deliver the project on time?' is a loaded question. In court, a question like this would qualify as the lawyer leading the witness. Lawyers learn to ask questions to which they *know* the answer: 'Mrs Fothergill, you were indeed standing over the body with the knife in your hand when the police arrived, were you not?' Let's leave that technique to the courtroom.

We must listen carefully because how we handle questions and non-questions as a presenter requires different tools and techniques.

Take control

Remember how we structure the ABCD introduction? Not only does ABCD get your audience listening, on board and interested (A – attention), because what you're saying is about them and what they will gain (B – benefits) and you are qualified to speak on this topic (C – credentials), it also sets their expectation as to what will happen. The D for direction allows you to steer your audience towards what they are expected to think, feel, say, do or know, and when you expect them to ask their questions. For example:

'Over the next fifteen minutes, I will focus on x, y and z so that you can have confidence in the team and see how we'll deliver this project on time and on budget. I've allowed ten minutes for questions at the end, so to keep to time, may I request you save your questions until then.'

This won't work every time and often people will still interrupt you, but it helps. You have a greater chance of staying in control than if you say, 'Please feel free to ask any questions as we go along.' With that, your chances of sticking to the time allowed and not having to say, 'Yes, I'm coming to that…' are slim.

Better to take control, if possible. Set up your talk or speech so that your audience knows *when* they can ask questions. It's good for you and it's good for them, too. Audiences need to know what's expected of them.

The power of the proxy

What if you don't get any questions? You get to the Q&A and all you hear is a deathly hush.

Don't panic. People need time, a few moments to reflect on what you said and process their questions. Some people may jump straight in, others need to think about what they want to say and build the courage to speak. Don't underestimate how nervous some people get about asking a question.

To get the ball rolling, you can use a proxy. This technique is often employed at conferences, but you can equally use it in your own presentations.

At a conference, the moderator will usually have two or three questions prepared for the speaker. Seasoned circuit speakers will always provide questions to the moderator, ones that they know they can handle and enjoy answering, and that will stimulate discussion.

Once one question comes in, it can prompt others to follow. The audience warms up, questions flow. If there are no questions, the moderator can then pose those you gave in advance.

If you are presenting, you can do your own version by asking a question to yourself, for example:

- 'One question people often raise on this topic…'
- 'I'm often asked…'

Another technique is to have a proxy in your audience, ready with a question to put to you on behalf of the audience. At conferences, I am often that proxy. The organisers, knowing that they can rely on me to say something(!), will ask before the session, 'Izzy, when we get to Q&A, would you ask a question?' I completely understand why they do it and I'm happy to oblige.

Sometimes they'll ask me to pose a question on a particular aspect so the speaker can be ready, other times they just leave it to me. If questions flow, I may not be needed. They know they can trust me to read the room.

Get your own proxy. Check with them beforehand, so they know to expect to ask a question. If I were the proxy, the speaker might say, 'We were talking about this only yesterday, Izzy. You asked what's most important to the board about this project.' The speaker now has a question they are ready to handle plus the involvement from the audience.

How to handle questions with confidence

This technique is for a question that, if written down, would have a question mark at the end. It's based on the way traffic lights – red, amber, green – *should* be followed, which is not as my African friends say optional, nor are they Christmas decorations as a colleague from Naples describes them. This is the Highway Code; we follow the rules:

- Red – Stop

- Amber – Get ready to go

- Green – Go

To encourage questions, think about what you say.

'Does anyone have a question?' How inviting is this? It's a closed question. If you use it in a clipped tone with your arms folded, you're really saying, 'I don't want any questions.'

Draw your audience in. 'We've allowed ten minutes for your questions, and I'd like to take those now.' At this point, a strange thing can happen: silence. Your audience may go inward, reflecting on what they've heard or searching through their notes, so it may take a few seconds before they work out their questions. Don't be surprised – or alarmed – if the room goes quiet. It doesn't mean there are no questions.

Stay calm, breathe; a question will probably come. If not, have your proxy options ready. When the questions do come, have your traffic lights to hand.

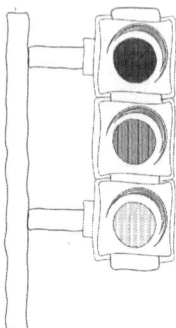

Red – STOP! – Repeat, rephrase, respect

Amber – Get ready and answer
(look out for your Achilles Heel)

Green – Get agreement

Red light – STOP!

When you hear a question, I want you to stop, just as you would if you were driving or crossing the road and the lights in front of you were red. Red light means stop. Pause. Give it time. Time to repeat and rephrase it, always respecting the question.

Other people may not have heard the question. They're still thinking about their own questions, so they may only catch half of it, or it may just be noise. For their benefit (as well as your own), repeat or rephrase the question.

You might be tempted to say, 'That's a good question' or 'That's a great question'. My advice: don't. That phrase tends to creep in when we get a question we don't know the answer to. If you say, 'That's a great question' to one, you are duty bound to say it to all – which can sound patronising. Alternatively, you say it to one and other people get miffed. They might think their question was better.

Unless you are speaking to only two or three people and the question is very clear, I recommend you repeat, rephrase and/or summarise what is asked. This is for everyone's benefit:

- It allows you to check that you've understood the actual question, not what you think the question is.

- You can explore the question in detail – there may be more to it. One question can sometimes hide another.

- It buys you time to consider your answer or for the person who asked the question to answer it for you. That's very useful and happens more than you might think, especially when the question was probably a point of view.

- Everyone else gets to hear the question and can therefore understand your answer. This avoids the same question being asked again later because it wasn't heard the first time, which is awkward for you and embarrassing for the questioner.

Even if the question appears to require a simple yes or no response, it's still helpful to repeat or rephrase it. For example, you could rephrase 'Will the project complete on time?' with 'Do you mean will the project complete by the end of Q2?' rather than just saying yes. The questioner might have thought it was due by end of Q1.

'How much will this cost?' Simple? Maybe not. Is the questioner talking capital expenditure or operating costs? This month? This quarter? Check, confirm and clarify so that you can give the questioner the best answer possible.

Always respect the question. You may get 'stupid' questions or someone asking the same thing in different ways. You may be frustrated, having explained something in detail, to get a naïve or dumb question. Tempting though it may be, avoid any disrespect by implying that they're not paying attention, for example:

- 'I think you'll find I've already covered that on slide 54' (you muppet). 'As I said previously...' (implication, you clearly weren't listening)

I remember a visit to a car showroom. After a long pitch by the sales rep (mostly technical, I was getting bored but was too polite to say), I asked, 'So what sort of mileage, roughly, will I get from driving this car?'

As quick as a flash, in a patronising drawl, 'Forty-three mpg on the urban cycle.' I'm surprised he didn't add 'duh' after the word cycle. OK, he knew his stuff, but I certainly didn't feel respected.

It's easy to forget red light. Even when I rehearse with delegates, they often jump straight to answer. Sometimes I have a red balloon or ball and wave it about.

You must practise this technique. Remember, red light means *stop*! Repeat, rephrase and always respect the question.

Amber – Get ready and answer

The red traffic light is your prompt to stop for the benefit of yourself and your audience. The amber light is your cue to get ready and *answer the question* – not what you'd like the question to be. That's a technique reserved for the more dodgy politicians or snake oil pedlars – 'I think the question you should be asking me is...'

Answer the question. Keep it short. Less is more. Don't go down a rat hole.

I remember attending a huge product launch for a new top-of-the-range laptop. After extolling its virtues and much excitement and music, the presenter asked the audience what questions they had. One of the first was, 'When can we expect to take delivery of the new laptops?' There was an answer: first shipments would be available at the end of Q1, March.

The speaker's actual response? 'We plan to deliver in Q1. Manufacturing has confirmed they can ship the first batches to our premium partners in March if orders are placed now, but we won't have much software ready until later in the year and we anticipate prices dropping, so...'

Oh dear. Result? No one placed an order.

Answer the question.

You also need to know your Achilles heel. According to Greek mythology, Achilles was the strongest warrior in the Trojan wars. However, he had a weak spot and that was his heel. As a child, he was held by his foot and dipped in the river Styx to make him invulnerable, but his heel didn't touch the magic water. When the Trojan prince Paris shot an arrow into his heel, Achilles died from the infection.

Every presentation has an Achilles heel, something that you would prefer your audience didn't ask about. You will be sensitive to your weakness, and like a magnet, you'll be drawn to it. It happens when I ski – if there is *one* small rock in the middle of a wide slope, I always seem to be drawn to it and fall over.

I was coaching a sales team who were pitching a multi-million deal to an international bank. Their Achilles heel was that due to export controls, they couldn't deliver directly to Germany – the country that was buying; they had to ship via Switzerland. This was normal at the time and caused no issue for customers, but the team worried it was a weak spot and might jeopardise the deal.

We rehearsed the pitch, and then practised how they would respond to questions and objections with me playing the prospective customer. Without warning, I went for the Achilles heel:

'May I just confirm,' I asked. 'You can deliver to Germany, can't you?'

The look on their faces in the rehearsal. Horror. Open mouths. Gulping for air.

'Er... well... yes, but no, we have to go via Switzerland...'

Whoaa! Listen to the question. Repeat, rephrase. The question was not 'Can you ship directly to Germany?' which they couldn't do. The question was, 'Can you deliver to Germany?' which they absolutely could. The equipment could have gone via Timbuktu as far as the customer was concerned, but the team members panicked when they heard a question that touched their Achilles heel, the weak spot in their pitch, and

I'd drawn their attention to it even more with my 'You can, can't you?'

That's why we practise and rehearse, even questions.

A tip for handling questions in person. It's natural to fix your eye contact on the person asking the question. It feels right. However, if you do, you risk not connecting with the rest of your audience. They may be rolling their eyes in frustration, and you miss it.

Ideally, spend 30–40% of your answer time with eye contact on the questioner, and the rest of the time working the room. Then you come back to the questioner to get agreement, which we will cover next.

Green – Get agreement

When you've answered the question, it's important that you close out. It's respectful, it's professional and shows that you have your audience's best interests at heart (remember our Trust Equation). I call this 'getting the green light'. It means you can proceed as you've checked in with your questioner.

It's easy to forget the red light and go straight to answer. It's also easy to forget the green light, but your response is much more effective if you return to the person who posed the question and ask, 'Does that answer it for you?' or 'Have I covered it?'

Some people may encourage you to move swiftly on after answering a question and take the next one. I don't. If you haven't answered their question to their satisfaction, you'll have a member of your audience stewing – or worse. How frustrated would you be if your question wasn't answered properly by a presenter, and you were then passed over? Cancel culture in action.

Getting the green light does run the risk of further discussion and you may need to manage that, but I would prefer you to do it and truly engage with your audience. Make it a habit not just for your benefit, but for your audience's. All you need to say is 'Is that OK?' or 'Does that make sense?' or 'I hope that answers your question for you…'

Questions versus objections

How do we handle the 'non-question'? Handling a question with my traffic light technique is straightforward. Dealing with a tricky audience member, less so.

'I don't see you being able to deliver this project on time.' This is an opinion, not a question, and what we're facing is a difference. As the speaker, I believe my team can deliver on time and on budget. This person isn't convinced. I see it one way, they see it another. There's a gap between us.

Think back to when you've faced resistance. If what the other person said to you was written down, there would be no question mark. How did you feel when you heard their objection? Threatened? Annoyed? Frustrated? Wanting to punch them? Probably not deep joy.

Recognise what resistance is: a gap in understanding between you and the person in your audience. You want to look to close that gap, but not by pushing back. Being right (in your view) or justifying your position simply won't work. As someone once said to me, 'Every time you're "right", someone loves you a little less.'

As the announcements say on the London Underground, 'Mind the gap'. For example:

- I think I'm the best candidate for the job; the interviewer doesn't see it that way.

- I think my team can deliver on time and on budget; the CEO isn't convinced.

- I believe my company's solution is good and we have the right experience; the buyer is not so sure.

How do you deal with the gap? Use APAC: *acknowledge* there is a gap, *probe* with genuine curiosity to understand why, *address* the gap, and then find a way to *close* it.

Acknowledge
Pause
'OK' or summarise their words
Emotion:
'I can understand you're being ...'

Confirm
Pause
'How do you feel about...?'
'Is that OK?'
'Does that go some way to addressing your concerns?'

No!

Probe
'Tell me more'
Ask questions (plural)
Listen, don't judge

Answer
Address
their concern
Feel, Felt, Found

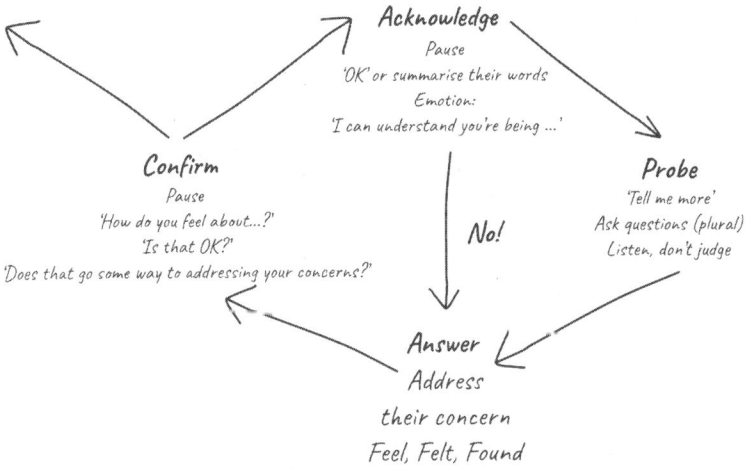

Step 1: Acknowledge there is a gap

Firstly, if you feel annoyed or frustrated at the push-back, breathe from your diaphragm so you have oxygen circulating and no build-up of carbon dioxide. That can make you light-headed.

Listen carefully – what did the objector *say*? What was the emotion behind the words? You must show that you are listening. Repeat and reframe the objection as with the red traffic light, show you respect their view and you care.

For example: 'OK, what I'm hearing is… It sounds as though…'

Through your response, you show empathy, that you're listening and their view is valid, however you may feel.

You might even agree with them. If the audience member says, 'We don't have the resources to deliver this project', your response may be, 'Yes, that's true. We don't have sufficient resources *right now*.' Showing that they could be right will get them on side – you're not immediately in conflict.

Step 2: Probe – explore the gap by asking questions

Your aim here is to understand what lies *behind* this gap. Why does the other person see something one way when you see it another? Rather than telling them why they're wrong – and pushing back – look to explore through your questions.

When we acknowledge that the other person might be right by saying, for example, 'Yes, we don't have all the resources right now', we show that we're listening. By agreeing with them, we're helping to neutralise the situation. It's no longer so confrontational.

Our questions might be:

- 'What do you see as the main barrier?'
- 'What would you need to see/have in place to be sure we can deliver?'

- 'If we can secure the resources, will you be comfortable supporting the project?'

To explore the gap, we must ask questions, plural. It's easy to ask one question and think that's enough. Be curious – understand *why* they see things differently. Sometimes, when we ask good questions, the objector may close the gap themselves.

Through your questions, you gain greater understanding of their view, why they see something the way they do. You can now provide other suggestions that address their real concern. In doing so, you build rapport with your audience, not conflict.

A great question to have ready is: 'What would you need to see to be sure I have/my team has the experience you're looking for?'

You might get a response like this: 'We'd need to see the CVs of each team member and be sure that they've worked on similar projects within the last eighteen months. We'd also really like to speak to a customer for whom you've done a project like ours – to be sure that you can deliver within the timescales.'

Now you know what you need to do, and all because you asked genuinely curious questions.

Step 3: Address the gap (and share a story)

We may not be able to convert our objector imme-diately, but greater understanding will help. If they could support us to get more resource (people or fund-ing), then we may be able to address their concern.

A story may be appropriate here, using the 5D struc-ture. We could share how we overcame a similar prob-lem (never the same, each one is unique) previously:

'Using this project to improve our organisation's skills in product management would be a great way forward. My team and I had a similar situation when I worked in my previous company xxx (first D: description).

'We wanted to run the project in-house and build capability (second D: desire), but we didn't have all the skills needed. Hiring wasn't possible because of headcount restrictions and the time it would have taken (third D: dilemma), so we sourced a specialist contractor for two months to support the project, dur-ing which time she trained up three team members in the new methodology (fourth D: delivered).

'This worked very well. The project was completed ahead of schedule, a first for us, while the team learned new skills and were then able to apply them to another project a few months later, saving us over $50,000 (fifth D: differentiator).'

When we hear resistance or spot a gap in understanding, it could be based on logic or emotion. We must listen carefully.

Compare these statements:

- 'I don't see how that can work for us.'
- 'I don't feel that's the right way forward for us.'

The first is based on logic and needs a logical response. The second is based on emotions and feelings, it requires a different response.

I love what I do. I get to travel to all sorts of interesting places and work with amazing people, but it can be tiring, especially when flights are delayed. It's a Friday night, I've battled through passport control, caught the bus and made it home. I slump into a chair, exhausted, moaning that no one appreciates my efforts, woe is me and so on, to which my husband replies:

'If it's making you that tired, stop travelling and training and do something else...'

'No, no. I love what I do!'

'Then stop complaining.'

My outburst is, of course, emotional, his response logical. I don't want to change my job – I just want some sympathy, attention and perhaps a glass of wine before dinner.

Listen carefully and spot the differences between a *logical* objection and an *emotional* one. It may be subtle, but adapting how you deal with each one will take you to new heights as a presenter.

'Feel, felt, found' is a technique to respond to emotional objections. This builds rapport and addresses the other person's emotional need. It can be used in the first person ('I' or 'myself'), in the third person (someone else) or third party (another organisation).

This statement is not a question: 'I don't feel comfortable with what you're suggesting.'

The word 'feel' tells us this is an emotional objection. The person is uncertain and it doesn't *feel* right. We think it is a good way forward, they don't. Responding with logic won't work, it's not about being right or wrong. It requires an emotional response.

We still acknowledge to show we've heard what they said, we still ask questions to understand what lies behind the objection and close the gap, but when we move to answer it, we use feel, felt, found.

We could say: 'I understand how you *feel*. I *felt* the same when I first looked at this, but what I *found* was...'

It might be even more powerful to use a third person or third party – describe a situation that we've experienced, using a story.

'I understand how you might be feeling. In fact, our MD felt uncomfortable when I first talked to her about this new approach. What she found was by working through the project plan and sharing the contractor information with weekly check-ins, we could stay on track, and it worked.'

Whether you use feel, felt, found in the first or third person, you are in effect using a story. You're sharing what you or someone else went through to show a way forward. You're allowing the person who's raised the objection to connect at a deeper emotional level, creating a sense of intimacy.

An important point: your story must be genuine. You can't make up feel, felt, found, but if you prepare for an objection, you can prepare your response, too.

Step 4: Close the gap – check and confirm that you've made progress

Having explored what lies behind the resistance, addressed the gap through our questions and answered it with logic or feel, felt, found (for emotion), we now check in to make sure that we've gone some way to closing it. Just as we did with the green traffic light.

When we check and confirm, we show that we have the other person's best interests at heart (low self-orientation from our Trust Equation). We use phrases such as:

- 'Does that make sense?'

- 'Does that go some way to addressing your concerns?'

- 'Could you see that working for you?'

- 'How would you feel about doing…?'

Note the tentative wording: 'Does that go some way to addressing your concerns?' People don't throw up their hands, confess they must be mad, clearly you are right and they've seen the light. They are cautious and may still not be totally convinced. Sometimes they don't want to lose face in front of their colleagues.

By saying, 'Does that go some way to addressing your concerns?' you make it easier for them to say 'Yes' or 'OK, but let's see how things go.' You've partly closed the gap; perhaps not entirely, but you've made progress.

When you check and confirm, either you'll get a yes (albeit tentative) or they'll continue to resist. If it's the latter, move back to Step 1, acknowledge and repeat the process.

FROM MY HANDS TO YOURS

Mindset

- Reflect on why you worry (if you do) about questions and objections. Reframe what a question or resistance is: an opportunity to engage with your audience, not a barrier.
- Recognise in your own mind that resistance is a gap in understanding. Focus on finding a way forward that will close the gap.
- Be aware that you can't stop how you might react, but you can choose your mindset for how you respond.

Toolset

- Prepare for questions and consider what resistance you may face.
- Use your traffic lights – stop (red light), answer (amber light) and get agreement (green light) – when asked a genuine question.
- Prepare with proxy questions or a physical proxy.
- Listen carefully to the question, they're not all equal. Use the red light to check your understanding.

- When there is no question mark after a question, it's resistance. Use acknowledge, probe, answer, confirm – APAC – to manage it.

- Don't panic and make a drama out of a crisis when you hear something that could be an Achilles heel. Recognise what it is – a weak spot – and handle it as you would any other question.

Skillset

- Get into the habit of using your traffic light technique for handling questions and your APAC tool for dealing with resistance. As always, practise in daily settings – a team meeting, a briefing – and rehearse your Q&A.

- Draw a picture of traffic lights on your notes or diamond, so you remember to use them.

- Practise. Rehearse. Video yourself and make sure you complete the traffic light sequence and all elements of APAC.

- Ask colleagues to come up with questions and challenges for you to practise with.

Conclusion

When I first started working on this book, my goal was clear: to help you present with presence and confidence. It's been quite a journey. With a toolset to support you at every stage of your speaking adventure, you're ready.

For those grappling with glossophobia, I want you to feel empowered with proven steps that will help you become a great speaker. However, this book isn't just for those who struggle with fear; it's also for the seasoned presenters seeking to elevate their skills. If you want more presence, the tools are right here. This book is the result of countless hours dedicated to learning, training, coaching, rehearsing and delivering presentations.

I remember the days when the thought of speaking in front of an audience filled me with dread. I watched in envy as others delivered their messages effortlessly, their confidence shining through. I longed for that ease – no shaky hands, no racing heart, no squeaky voice – but here's the truth: those seemingly fearless speakers didn't get there by chance. It was through practice, learning, and invaluable feedback along the way.

If you were fortunate enough to participate in 'show and tell' during your school years, your teachers and parents set you on a path to success. For the rest of us, public speaking takes deliberate effort. We need our recipes, our frameworks and, most importantly, the time to plan and prepare, seizing every opportunity to practise.

How do we improve? Some say practice makes perfect; I believe practice cultivates habits (not always good ones) and progress. To be the best we can, we must welcome feedback – whether through scrutinising videos of ourselves (remember, if it's on your phone, only you need to watch it and you can delete it) or through inviting colleagues, managers and mentors to observe us. Growth comes from stepping outside our comfort zone and trying out new tools. If we're too comfortable doing something, we're probably not learning.

In each chapter of the book, I have summarised the mindset, toolset, skillset approach that I use when I coach and train others. This is my way to hand over to you all that I've learned.

You now have Izzy's diamond, and if you follow the link here https://masterclass.co.uk/the-diamond you can access an interactive PDF version that you can use again and again. Start your outline – topic in the middle, audience at the top, outcomes at the bottom (what you want your audience to think, feel, say, do or know) – and in minutes you will have a plan. Transfer it to the diamond, and your structure and timings are laid out for you.

Prepare your ABCD introduction to engage your audience from the get-go. Then dip in to the techniques you need to build stories, have presence, warm up your voice, look your best and handle questions and tricky audiences.

Let's challenge ourselves to be the very best we can and unlock our potential as powerful presenters.

Resources

Books and articles

Bains, S, 'Jo Brand says being spat at and fat-shaming hecklers are nothing compared to abuse she suffered in first job' (*Mirror*, 4 April 2024) www.mirror.co.uk/3am/celebrity-news/jo-brand-recalls-horror-experience-32497984, accessed 12 March 2025

Crystal, D, *The Gift of the Gab: How eloquence works* (Yale University Press, 2017)

Heath C; Heath, D, *Made to Stick: Why some ideas take hold and others come unstuck* (Arrow, 2008)

Lee, H, *To Kill a Mockingbird* (William Heinemann, 1960)

Maister, DH; Galford, R; Green, CH, *The Trusted Advisor* (Simon & Schuster, 2002)

TED Talks

Cuddy, A, 'Your body language may shape who you are' (TEDGlobal, June 2012) www.ted.com/talks/amy_cuddy_your_body_language_may_shape_who_you_are, accessed 11 March 2025

Kleinberger, R, 'Why you don't like the sound of your own voice' (TEDxBeaconStreet, November 2017) www.ted.com/talks/rebecca_kleinberger_why_you_don_t_like_the_sound_of_your_own_voice?language=en, accessed 11 March 2025

LeBorgne, W, 'Vocal branding beyond words: How your voice shapes your communication' (TEDxUCincinnati, February 2018) www.ted.com/talks/wendy_leborgne_vocal_branding_beyond_words_how_your_voice_shapes_your_communication_image, accessed 11 March 2025

Russell, C, 'Looks aren't everything. Believe me, I'm a model' (TEDxMidAtlantic, October 2012) www.ted.com/talks/cameron_russell_looks_aren_t_everything_believe_me_i_m_a_model, accessed 12 March 2025

Treasure, J, 'How to speak so that people want to listen' (TEDGlobal, June 2013) www.ted.com/talks/julian_treasure_how_to_speak_so_that_people_want_to_listen, accessed 11 March 2025

Acknowledgements

So many people have made this book possible – Suzy Siddons who was there at the start of Masterclass. Our incredible team of trainers and coaches – each with their unique skills, experiences and generosity: Ben Harvey, Caron Darwood, Colette Ashby, Deborah Hall, Diana Shaw, Gail Bennett, Claire Portman, Emma Church, James Auden, Jane Owens, Mark Perry, Martin Kahn, Mary Foster, Mike Pick, Paul Kenny, Paul Dubois, Ric Hayden, Rob Schilling, Steve Torjussen, Paul Burton, William Galton, Theresa Caragol, Helen Bouchami, Dugald Christie-Johnston, April Redshaw, Lorraine Bevan, Brad Solomon, Alison Rushworth, Derek Ayling, Tim Robertson, Michelle Rosenberg and Morgan James.

Sharon Fennell – who helped develop the whole concept of Powerful Presence and who is a brilliant and inspiring trainer. Kelly Bodman, always happy to test drive new ideas and provide feedback. Paul Russell, creative thinker and sounding board and now an author too. The late wonderful Steven van Agt who encouraged me to write my first book and who was always so supportive. Luan Wise who continues to challenge me and who is now on her eighth book (I've got some catching up to do).

All the politicians I've worked with over the years and especially Sir Ed Davey for being generous in his foreword to this book. I've learned so much from all of you.

To the thousands of people I've had the privilege to train and coach over the last thirty years – you've taught me more than you could ever know. I've been so lucky to have a career (if you can call it that) where I've been able to continue to learn and develop new ideas.

To all at Rethink Press for their endless patience and encouragement – I couldn't do it without you.

And to my amazing team at Masterclass who have put up with me disappearing to get this finished. Especially to Catherine Wilson, Laura Feminier, Gemma Pepper, Michael Sloane, Sue Allen and our chairman and my mentor, Stan Patey.

And, of course, the cost centres or should I say children, Josie, Tom and Ellie – all finding your own successful way in the world – along with Julian and little Artemis. I'm so proud of you.

Finally, my husband Martin who's put up with me all these years and who does, regularly, provide a glass of Bandol rosé wine before dinner in response to my emotional outbursts. Thank you.

The Author

Founder of Masterclass Training, Isobel graduated from the University of Surrey and spent a year working in France before joining the computer company, Digital Equipment, on their graduate sales programme. The last thing she expected was to become a salesperson, and least of all in technology.

She now leads a team of over seventy trainers and coaches and has worked with hundreds of global organisations in the design and delivery of training programmes in management and leadership, sales and business development and in presentation and communication skills. Her first book, *Natural Business*

Development, became a best seller when published in 2020 and is based on her belief that if we reframe what selling is all about – being curious and helping clients to solve problems – we can make it easy for them to want to buy from us.

Masterclass is a global training partner for Kouzes & Posner, The Leadership Challenge working with the Five Practices of Exemplary Leaders and the Leadership Practices 360 Inventory. Isobel and her team have delivered hundreds of programmes incorporating this approach.

Clients include PricewaterhouseCoopers, IBM, Trend Micro, Oxford Economics, Analysys Mason, Mace Group, DLA Piper, AvisBudgetGroup, BNP Paribas, Tripadvisor as well as the Probation Service, Fire and Rescue Services, many NHS Trusts and Central and Local Government.

Isobel has trained politicians and people in the public domain, helping them to present with confidence and develop their gravitas as speakers. She has appeared many times on TV as a presentation skills 'pundit' advising on image, impact and personal presence and is a former columnist for Training Journal.

She is married to Martin and has three children – or cost centres as she prefers to describe them. Her younger daughter has cerebral palsy and as a result Isobel has served as a Regional Chair for Scope, the disability charity.

When she's not working, you'll probably find her walking a Bernese Mountain dog.

⊕ https://masterclass.co.uk

◼ www.facebook.com/masterclasstrainingltd

◼ www.linkedin.com/company/masterclass

◼ https://x.com/Masterclass_T

◎ www.instagram.com/masterclass.training